PRAISE

"A new window on the much-neglected invisible dimensions of our humanity. Great reading."
~ Wayne W. Dyer, *The Shift*

"Describes what each of us can do to remove the blocks to our own creativity, and thus more fully express our essential being."
~ Shakti Gawain, *Creative Visualization*

"Combines insight, experience, and ancient wisdom. Not only worth reading but referencing and studying."
~ Hugh Prather, *Notes to Myself*

"A wonderfully lucid and intelligent book, full of fascinating insight."
~ Gabrielle Roth, *Maps to Ecstasy*

"Brings the magical world of existence into our everyday lives."
~ Lynn Andrews, *Medicine Woman*

"Offers new perspectives on the process of rebirthing spiritual insight."
~ Terence McKenna, *The Archaic Revival*

Spirit Guides

Other Books by The Author

Write Starts: Prompts, Quotes and
Exercises to Jumpstart Your Creativity

Write From the Heart: Unleashing the
Power of Your Creativity

Writing Spiritual Books: A Bestselling
Writers Guide to Successful Publication

The Lens Of Perception: A Users'
Guide to Higher Consciousness

Follow Your Bliss: Discovering
Your Inner Calling and Right Livelihood,
with Susan J Sparrow

Spirit Animals And The Wheel of Life:
Earth-Based Spirituality for Everyday Living

Spirit Circle: A Novel of Shamanic Revelation

Zuni Fetishes: Using Native American Objects
for Meditation, Reflection & Insight

Invitation to Success: Nobel Acton's
Eleven Habits of Creativity and Innovation

The Holotropic Mind, with Stanislav Grof

Spirit Guides

Hal Zina Bennett
with Susan J Sparrow

TENACITY PRESS

Copyright © 2002, 2010 by Hal Zina Bennett

Published by Tenacity Press
1-800-738-6721

All rights reserved. This book may not be
reproduced in any form, or in any part, without
written permission from the publisher,
except by a reviewer who may quote
passages in a review, or by an
author of a non-fiction work who may
use excerpts of up to 50 words
for books on similar subjects.
The author allows fair use if clear
acknowledgment is noted.

Readers are cautioned that this book is not
intended to replace advice or treatment for
any health condition whatsoever.

ISBN 1-4536-2353-1
4th Edition
10 9 8 7

Dedicated to that quiet,
seeking spirit within each
of us, constantly reaching
for a greater truth.

Acknowledgments

No book would be possible without the efforts of a great many people behind the scenes: editors, graphic artists, printers, office workers who supervise printing and shipping, book distributors, book sellers, and finally the readers.

There are many teachers who helped to open my mind to the material I describe in this book. Probably the first was the imaginary friend of my earliest childhood who was the first to tell me: "All is not as it appears." Though he often left me with more questions than answers, I also found an odd comfort in his presence and trusted his wisdom.

I want to acknowledge my life partner and wife, Susan J Sparrow, the love of my life, who has held a light for me all the years we have been together.

Finally, no list of this kind would be complete without mentioning our children, grandchildren, parents, siblings, friends, cousins, in-laws and extended family members, all of us reminders of the larger whole of which we are all a part.~

Contents

Acknowledgements

Introduction - p. 1

The Nature of Spirit Guides - p. 11

A Glimpse of the Greater Reality – p. 27

Lifelong Spirit Companions – p. 49

Meeting Your Spirit Guides – p. 67

Making Peace With Inner Critics – p. 81

Journeying for Spirit Guides – p. 91

Choices on the Spiritual Path – p. 101

Bibliography – p. 115

About the Authors – p. 116

Introduction

When I wrote the first edition of this book, over a decade ago, I did so because I'd received hundreds of requests for an easy to read book with clear instructions for working with spirit guides, a book with stories that would illustrate how these guides might be useful in everyday life. This turned out to be a challenge because I didn't want to repeat stories and examples I'd written in other books but if I were to tell the truth about my experience with spirit guides this was the only way I could do it. I asked some of my readers and students who were familiar with my work what they thought I should do. Would it be okay to repeat stories that were relevant, though they'd been published in other of my books?

I found overwhelming support for the idea of putting into one place those stories which authenticated breakthroughs in my own use of spirit guides, even though they might be repeats. There was total agreement that no book I'd write on this subject would be complete without these anecdotes. People wanted a book that made the subject highly accessible and personal--simple, straight-forward and real. To the best of my ability, and with Susan's encouragement and support, I have followed that advice.

What you'll find in this book, along with easy to follow instructions for getting your own guides, are the stories of the three key turning points that made spirit guides so important for me. I have woven these together with new information about the importance of such guides in all our lives and why there is renewed interest in them now. In addition, I have added a new chapter, *Choices on the Spiritual Path*, which presents brand new material that I have never published elsewhere in any form.

Ancient Wisdom In the Electronic Age

Our interest in spirit guides is perhaps as old as humanity itself. Throughout recorded history, and on virtually every continent, we find examples of how people have worked with spirits to assist them in their daily lives. Primarily, they have always given us access to the inner world of the spiritual and *imaginal* realms. They help to shift our perceptions from the world of our senses to the invisible reality of thought, emotion and spirit.

Today there are business people, scientists, artists, teachers, salespeople, doctors, college professors, psychotherapists, ministers, priests, rabbis, and health professionals who turn to their spirit guides for assistance on a regular basis. Many people learning how to use inner guides for the first time have remarked that after learning about them, they realized they had been accessing this source of knowledge unconsciously most of their lives. In most instances, they had just done it automatically, without an awareness of how to do it at will. After learning about spirit guides, however, they are able to access their spirit guides by choice rather than only serendipitously. That is the main purpose of this book.

One of the insights we get after learning about spirit guides is that the boundaries of the self extend far beyond our immediate physical environment. We begin to experience new perceptions of the self. We see that we are spiritually linked with people halfway around the world, and with those who lived hundreds, even thousands of years ago. We begin to see that we emerge from, and are the expressions of, a single consciousness that is limited by neither time nor space. We are just as affected by events in the distant past as we are by those in the immediate present. And in some cases, our spirit guides even give us partial access to the future.

For most of us, insights provided by spirit guides can seem quite detached from our daily lives, where most of our attention is focused on events right in front of us. Yet, psychologists and spiritual teachers warn us that unless we do get in touch with the spiritual and psychological truths that profoundly influence our lives, we are not free to make truly informed and viable choices.

Throughout western society we are undergoing a major shift in our understanding of the self. We begin to see that the human body is not merely a mass of protoplasm whose movements are run by the brain but is, rather, an energy being, a center of vibrancy, whose waves radiate out beyond the immediate environment through time and space. Moreover, these waves respond to and interact with an infinite variety of other waves, just as the constantly shifting, interacting currents of the ocean do.

We are coming to see that our human forms are singular manifestations of a larger energy being—call it Universal Light, the Life Force, God, or whatever other term you wish to apply—and that we in fact exist within a body of energy that extends infinitely throughout our own planet and out into infinite space. The energy of which we are a part transcends space and time, connecting us all, regardless of where or even when we have lived.

The Noosphere and Spirit Guides

Jesuit paleontologist Teilhard de Chardin, described a "thinking layer," or noosphere, that envelopes the Earth. This layer is activated, in part, by each and every conscious being that is or ever was. In effect, we are each like one cell in a giant brain, contributing to a whole that is too large for any of us to fully comprehend, Teilhard says:

This noosphere is just as extensive and coherent as any other sphere of our planet, be it the atmosphere, the lithosphere, the hydrosphere, or the biosphere. Outside and above the biosphere, the noosphere constitutes the thinking layer, which, since its germination at the end of the Tertiary period, has spread over and above the world of plants and animals.

As we become increasingly familiar with the use of spirit guides, we connect with more and more of this thinking layer of our planet. And we begin to understand our part in it, the implied responsibility of participating in life at that level, and that we receive much for opening ourselves more fully to it. We see that we are no more separated from the Earth's noosphere than are our individual brain cells separated from the totality of our brains. Individual consciousness seamlessly merges with and emanates from the noosphere.

There's a wonderful quote of Lewis Thomas' that describes this relationship very well:

We still argue the details, but it is conceded almost everywhere that we are not the masters of nature that we thought ourselves; we are as dependent on the rest of life as are the leaves or midges or fish. We are part of the system. One way to put it is that the Earth is a loosely formed, spherical organism, with all its working parts linking in symbiosis.

It is my belief that only by gaining greater knowledge about, and skill with, the contents of our inner worlds, that we can hope to solve the chief problems of today, that is, whether or not we will destroy our planet, render it uninhabitable for life as we know it, or we will fully embrace it and help it flourish so that it will support and enjoy our future generations. We have the technology to go either way. But the choice about how to use that power may or may not be a rational one. Our inner worlds often work in mysterious ways, and we must learn to accept and apply the wisdom we are offered from the inner world. Otherwise, we are destined to repeat the errors of the past and fail to see our potential for the future.

The more familiar we become with our inner worlds, and the more we honor our connectedness with the noosphere, the more we are likely to protect and love that which nurtures us, the Earth herself. And the more connected we feel with the cosmos, the more we will receive the bounties of Mother Earth and the spirit of life that is the special gift of this wondrous planet.

The more you explore the world of spirit guides, the more you'll discover a certain familiarity about the territory they inhabit. In fact, as this familiarity grows your visits to this place within your consciousness will be like coming home.

Through our use of spirit guides we come to know new levels of comfort within ourselves, along with a growing appreciation for our spiritual nature. Spirit guides are literally companions and counselors who can communicate with us in simple, direct ways, tapping the infinite wisdom of the noosphere.

The wealth of knowledge we find through spirit guides can be applied in any number of ways—in developing richer personal relationships, in improving emotional and physical well being, in having an increased ability to face problems and find solutions in everyday life, in creative endeavors, and in tapping into the powers of what some people call the sixth sense, that is, the intuitive or psychic side of our beings that connects us with the greater whole.

Carl Jung, recognized as one of the modern world's foremost leaders in the exploration of human consciousness, once called this inner world *the greatest of all cosmic wonders.*

Spirit guides are a very normal and natural part of the human experience. As you gain more practice with them, you will probably discover, as thousands of others have, that that, as a very young child, you had an imaginary playmate. Or perhaps you had a favorite doll you talked with, seeking counsel and comfort when parents or playmates hurt your feelings. They in fact were your earliest teachers.

As you grew older, you may have adopted heroes—movie stars, rock stars, artists, characters from fiction, or even the memory of a favorite relative—who also served this purpose. In quiet times, feeling the need for their strength, their company, or their counsel, you allowed yourself to daydream, to inwardly converse with these friends of the inner landscape.

Mystery of the Source

The mystery about the source of spirit guides remains but we do know that there are many records of conversations with such beings, most of them highly beneficial, which appear in literature, psychology, philosophy, music, science, and religious texts throughout the world. In the final analysis our explanation of the source of the inner guides—where they come from or what they represent in the world—is less important than their message. Millions of people, throughout the ages, have found them to be the source of wisdom, comfort and revelation that clearly improve the quality of life.

However you choose to use your guides, bear in mind that just as in any other personal relationship in your life, you are responsible for choosing to accept or reject the information they provide. But do not understand them too quickly. There is a wonderful story told by Sun Bear, who brought us so many valuable teachings from the Native American traditions. He tells about a spirit guide he had who was the reincarnation of a great warrior who'd lived centuries before. Sun Bear had great respect for this guide but each time he followed the spirit guide's advice Sun Bear got into trouble. Bewildered by this, Sun Bear went to his mortal teacher and told him what was happening. His teacher, a wise old medicine man, listened to Sun Bear's story with interest. When the story was done the old man turned to his student and said, simply, "Dead don't necessarily make you wise!"

The moral of this story is obvious: Spirit guides, like any other persons in our lives, are not infallible. Get to know your guides by contacting and communicating with them on a regular basis for a month or two before you start following their advice and counsel. The most enlightened of them will not prescribe a path for you, any more than the most enlightened counselor in our outer lives would. The most valuable information they provide will come through as flashes of insight or as gentle suggestions that will help you make subtle changes in the way you view your own life. Always keep Sun Bear's advice in mind, that being in a spiritual form rather than a mortal one doesn't automatically make your counselor wise or infallible.

With these considerations in mind, go forward on your journey to the world of spirit guides with a sense of adventure, exploration and play. Probe the mysteries of this realm with healthy skepticism but allow your heart and your mind to stay open to the many benefits it offers.

Just as in our daily lives in the physical world, we are most open to both the joys and the special moments of profundity when we remember to bring along the best of our own humor and humility. These are prerequisites for any spiritual seeker since they remind us that in our present lives, as physical beings, our egos as well as our five senses will limit what we can know of the universe. Just as the Bible tells us, within our human limitations we can only *see through a glass darkly*. We depend on divine inspiration to occasionally find the most translucent spots in the glass.

Spirit guides can provide us with these glimpses beyond the finite limits of the physical realm. At best they can point to tiny windows that give us a view of the mysteries beyond the world of the senses. What our spirit guides offer is surely worth our further exploration, for they can provide piercing insights that confirm our spiritual identity and provide insightful guidance that just might improve our everyday lives.~

The Nature of Spirit Guides

Thoughts are like animals in the forest, or people in a room, or birds in the air... If you should see people in a room, you would not think that you had made those people, or that you were responsible for them...
~C.G. Jung, attributed to his spirit guide Philemon

Science tells us that we ourselves generate our thoughts, our fantasies, our dreams and even our epiphanies. Growing up in the scientific tradition, as most of us have, we are tempted to dismiss talk about spirit guides or guardian angels, which belong to that mystical realm, as wistful thinking, if not sheer madness. Yet, there are those like C.G. Jung, one of the most highly acclaimed psychologists of the past two centuries (note the quote I have included above) who thoroughly believed that such entities were real and that they represented a source of wisdom beyond the scope of our everyday consciousness.

To clarify, the above quote was part of Philemon's (spirit guide) explanation when Jung asked him to explain what he was. Philemon essentially told him two things--that thoughts had lives of their own and were not merely a person's creation, and that spirit guides, such as Philemon, also had identities separate from the brain of the person they served.

Most of us have had at least some experience with these entities we call spirit guides. Maybe there was a moment when we thought we heard an inner voice advising us about something we were about to do. Or in a somnolent, dreamy moment we had the impression that someone was nearby comforting us when we were blue or encouraging us to go forward when we were stalled with self-doubt. While we might have had such experiences in childhood, and perhaps even in adulthood, the encounter was fleeting. Try as we might, we can't seem to call these kinds of experiences into our consciousness at will. At best, they appear serendipitously, then slip away the moment we realize what's happened.

When I was a small boy growing up in Michigan, I had an imaginary friend I called Alex. He was like a trusted older brother, eight or ten years my senior, and infinitely wiser than I in the ways of the world. When Alex was with me, we talked. Walking down the street in the suburban neighborhood where I lived, we carried on lengthy inner dialogues, and to me Alex was as real as any other person in my life.

My parents were at least tolerant when I told them about Alex though I am certain that had they understood how important he was in my daily life they might have been more concerned. Where I grew up, the idea of "talking to yourself" was not considered to be healthy behavior, to put it mildly. My parents' reaction, at worst, was to indulge me, treating my stories about my imaginary friend as "cute make-believes" that I would eventually outgrow.

I don't believe that my experience is unique. Over the years, I've taught thousands of people about the use of spirit guides. Time and time again, I hear stories similar to mine, where the childhood contacts with these guides were profound, yet were discouraged by well meaning adults or by older children. It is for this reason that I relate my own experiences, to assure readers that what they may have encountered in their own early lives around these guides was not unique.

If my parents indulged me in my imaginary friendship with Alex, my peers were less than kind. After suffering through the jibes of my playmates about "the little man who wasn't there," I found that I was better off not mentioning him at all. I kept him to myself. He comforted me when I was afraid. And even when I was six or seven years old he began tutoring me in ideas that no other older person in my life had ever discussed.

Alex was the first to point out to me that the physical world in which we live is not at all what it appears to be, that there was a much greater reality beyond this one, indeed responsible for this one, that I would one day come to see more clearly. He taught me to contemplate the infinite, instructing me to gaze at the stars in the evening sky and ponder the mysteries.

When pets in the neighborhood had babies, or when human mothers did, he focused my attention on the miracle of the life spirit that animated these new beings. Every new birth was a reminder that there was a power far greater than any human being, greater even than Nature herself. And everything I experienced, even my own thoughts, was an expression of this power.

Alex did not teach with words except to instruct me where and how to look for the truth: To look beyond the stars into infinite space. To look upon physical existence as a curtain, behind which was a larger truth. To look beyond the corporeal reality of a newborn, miraculous though this might be, to catch a glimpse of the Source that animates all. Alex' gentle coaching was the only metaphysical instruction I ever received in my childhood. Indeed, I was in my mid-twenties before I discovered that there were regular people in the world who discussed such things and took them seriously!

Gradually, as the pressures of my peers increased, I pushed my thoughts of Alex to the back of my mind, knowing it was somehow not acceptable. As I did so, Alex disappeared from my life, at least on a conscious level. Though it was I who abandoned him, I felt rebuffed and rejected, mourning his departure, though I did not understand this at the time. It was only years later, in psychotherapy, that I realized that what my parents had attributed to "moodiness" was actually a grieving for this important friend who was gone from my life.

It was not until I was in my twenties, when I was introduced to the writings of C.G. Jung, that I renewed my interest in spirit guides. Jung's work gave at least a hint of support and confirmation for my experiences with these elusive entities. Even so, I did not immediately let beings such as Alex back into my life. Jung spoke of the *anima* and *animus*, figures who appear in our unconscious, and which seem to us to be autonomous, that is, spirit beings whose personalities are separate from our own.

Jung said that the *anima* and *animus* were "not a question of anything metaphysical." Yet, he also admitted that the spirits or inner guides could be "as rich and strange as the world itself," and that as we begin "making them conscious we convert them into bridges to the unconscious."

For Jung, the *anima* and *animus* represented male and female functions, or personal characteristics that, for highly individualized reasons, were important to the person's overall vision of life. He pointed out that these beings and their functions had been noted by people in so-called primitive societies for perhaps tens of thousands of years.

It is interesting to note here that while reading the work of the Northern Cheyenne philosopher and shaman, Hyemeyohsts Storm, I would come upon these words: "Within every man there is the Reflection of a Woman, and within every woman there is the Reflection of a Man. Within every man and woman there is also the Reflection of an Old Man, an Old

Woman, a Little Boy, and a Little Girl."

Here, in the cosmologies of the Native American shaman, was further validation for spirit beings who communicate with us, and make their presence known through our consciousness. While Storm's insights intrigued me, I was primarily interested in western psychology at the time, and sought answers in Jung.

Jung taught me that as important as the functions or characteristics associated with the *anima* might be to us, we could not, or had not yet allowed ourselves to incorporate them into our personalities. So, at least on one level, these beings were manifestations, or offshoots, of our own psychology. An *anima* might embody characteristics that we considered distasteful, and which we could not accept as part of our own personality. Or we might reject it for what others might view as positive reasons. For example, an *anima* might embody a sense of self-power that we could not imagine ourselves possessing because to do so would mean that we would have to give up the security of a dependency on a parent or other loved one. In order to have these characteristics in our lives without fully owning them, we invented these spirits of the unconscious so that we could have some of the benefits of these characteristics without fully incorporating them into our personality.

To maintain our separateness from these characteristics and, at the same time, experience a sense of completeness in our outer world, Jung postulated, we might seek relationships with real people who matched, or as closely as possible matched the anima that lived within our unconscious. However, there were dangers in seeking the real world double of these spirits; people in the outer world could never quite fill the bill. They would be mere stand-ins who would leave us frustrated and bewildered. In addition, therapeutic work with people who attempted to do this, Jung found, revealed that the anima might defend its territory like a jealous lover or an overprotective parent, acting hurt or angry whenever we approached a person in the real world who might replace them. In that case, our emotional involvement with the *anima* or *animus* might result in our rejecting those persons in the outer world who threatened to replace the inner guide.

Jung believed that we could transform these guides from being sources of conflict in our lives to becoming real helpers. And one did that by speaking to the *animus,* and asking it questions such as why it was present in our life. For example, Allen, a friend of mine who went through Jungian analysis, reported having difficulty maintaining lasting relationships with the women in his life. He desperately wanted a stable relationship but any time he got close to a woman he liked he began acting in an offensive "chauvinistic" manner that literally drove her away. Though he intellectually understood what he was doing, and did not like himself when he was being chauvinistic, he could do nothing to stop himself.

In the course of his work with the Jungian therapist, Allen discovered that he had an inner guide who was a middle aged woman called Alice. Alice embodied all the human values that he had been taught were *feminine*. Though he felt a need for these feminine qualities in his life, he was unable to allow himself to consider them as elements of his own personality because, according to his father's values, this would have made him a sissy.

Allen eventually discovered that Alice was jealous of his relationships with the real women in his life, and it had been as a result of protecting Alice that he had manifest the chauvinistic behavior that drove away his prospective lovers.

Eventually, Allen started talking directly with Alice, treating her as if she was an actual person in his life. He told her that she must stop interfering with other relationships in his life. He went through a period of feeling guilty for doing this. But he realized that as an adult he had every right to determine who and what entered his consciousness. Soon after this, Allen did establish a successful relationship with a woman, and was eventually happily married.

Following his laying the law down to Alice, this *anima* eventually adopted a helpful role in Allen's life. He turned to her whenever he wanted guidance in emotional matters. It was, after all, the woman's job to take care of such matters--or so he had been led to believe by his parents. In time, Alice was transformed from being a source of conflict in his emotional relations to being a real helper, as Alice herself took on some of the strong male qualities Allen was developing.

One rather interesting aside is that after he was married, Allen became interested in cooking, and it soon became a deeply satisfying creative outlet--though it had been assigned to the woman's world in his father's eyes. When he was cooking, Allen said, he always had a strong sense of Alice's presence, as though she was helping him and fulfilling her own enjoyment of the culinary arts through him. He was now finding real pleasure in expressing the female aspects of his personality.

Beyond Anima and Animus

Jung as well as other psychologists have noted that there are other entities that can appear in our consciousness like the anima or animus but which are not products of our ego or personality. These may appear spontaneously in dreams, or through the use of active imagination (guided imagery or visualization), but in no way do their histories appear to be related to our own emotional struggles. In fact, they appear to be quite separate from the person perceiving them. For example, "channeled" entities such as Seth, made popular by the books of Jane Roberts, appear to be quite outside the everyday realms of the person receiving their words, would have to be viewed as something other than *anima* or *animus*.

It was in his memoirs that Jung described a conversation he had with his own spirit guide, Philemon, who was this latter kind of being. It is from his own comments that I drew the epigram for this chapter. I quote this in its entirety now:

> *I observed clearly that it was he (Philemon) who spoke, not I. He said I treated thoughts as though I generated them myself, but in his view thoughts were like animals in the forest, or people in a room, or birds in the air, and added, 'If you should see people in a room, you would not think that you had made those people, or that you were responsible for them.' It was he who taught me psychic objectivity, the reality of the psyche... He confronted me in an objective manner, and I understood that there is something in me which can say things that I do not know and do not intend.* (*From* Memories, Dreams, Reflections)

Upon reading this passage, and others concerning spirit guides in Jung's life, conflicts I had about my own childhood guide began to diminish. And I had a whole new set of questions to ask Alex, my tutor in the metaphysical realm.

Inner Guides As Teachers

As I began following Jung's model, I found that my task with at least some of the inner guides I encountered became one of accepting their importance in my inner life, and then allowing myself to learn from them, setting up the same kinds of sometimes skeptical, sometimes fully trusting relationships that I had with people in my outer world. And I found, indeed, that as I grew to know them, to recognize and accept their human strengths and weaknesses, my own personality took on their functions, just as it had done for the man in the above example. I could own the functions of character they represented.

In the 1970's I happened upon the research of Elmer and Alyce Green, published in their book *Beyond Biofeedback.* Their bio-feedback research, through the Menninger Foundation, made it clear that: "the unconscious mind did not distinguish between an imagined and a real experience." That which was imagined could have as dramatic affects on the body and the conscious mind as that which was experienced in the real world through the senses.

What bearing did this discovery have on inner guides? For me it was a great revelation; it suggested to me that in the final analysis it did not matter what the inner guides really were. The unconscious mind, which psychologists and neurophysiologists agree is the dominant force in our lives, experiences these persona just as it does any other *people* in our lives.

Given their potential affects on us, the first question that came to my mind was this: How can I recognize an *anima,* or for that matter a spirit guide, who may be misadvising me, or giving me wrong information, in order to protect her own interests? How could I determine who could be trusted and who couldn't in this inner world? I concluded that whether they were real or imagined, each one of us has a responsibility to weigh the value of whatever these beings bring to our lives. Sometimes they are right, sometimes wrong. Sometimes they were kind, sometimes cruel.

Whether they are real or not, one has to treat them as being, after all, only human, just as capable of vanity and folly and error as the rest of us. But I would have to live through many adventures, and a few misadventures, before I'd begin to understand how to make use of spirit guides, that there would be a particular path I would find that would carry me through this metaphysical wilderness.

Learning To Live Outside the Boundaries

In the 1960s, I was, like many others of my generation, experimenting with mind-altering drugs and entheogens. During a long stay in Mexico I took mescalin, in the form of magic mushrooms, with a person I would now call a shaman, though I did not know that name at the time. An entirely new vision of life opened up to me, one I did not understand, and since the shaman and I had no common language--he being an Indian, me being a gringo from north of the border--I could not get answered the myriad of questions pouring through my mind.

When I returned to the states, I continued to pursue this new vision of my life, and began taking peyote and LSD with another shaman I met, this time a man of Cherokee and Irish descent who I met in California.

Thanks to peyote, I began to see how my inner world colored and gave shape to my outer world, just as Alex had taught. With my shaman-teacher, the elusive world of inner consciousness became increasingly tangible and viable. Indeed, during long hallucinatory episodes, I saw and spoke with people who had previously appeared only in my inner world. Now these people took on separate identities, including what appeared to be real physical bodies in the external world. It was as though I had projected mental holograms from my inner world to the outer one. Yet, these people clearly were separate from me. When they spoke I knew their words had not come from my own mind; like Alex, the spirit guide of my childhood, they said and did things that I could not predict.

At first puzzled and frightened by these apparitions who now seemed so real to me, my shaman friend explained that they were spirit guides, beings from my inner world, and that they were in fact autonomous, real and separate from me. He encouraged me to speak with them, which I did. As I spoke with them, sometimes aloud, sometimes only inwardly, I recognized that they had always been a part of me, that they had lived in my consciousness, appearing in my dreams and daydreams, for as long as I could remember. I saw that they had presences as real to me and as separate from me, as those of my friends and acquaintances in the physical world. Granted, there was a difference between the two worlds, that is, the physical and the ethereal, but one was no less real than the other. I saw that the inner world figures had a lot to do with how I operated in the world; my interests, fears, likes and dislikes all related to my relationships with them. In fact, this was the first time I began to understand how my success in life was often more profoundly affected by the inner world reality than by the outer one.

When the peyote wore off, some twenty hours

later, I discussed what I had experienced with my shaman friend. He smiled and nodded, his face placid and maybe a little bemused, as though all my new insights were common knowledge--which to him they were. I wanted explanations. If he had any, he wasn't interested in giving them. In the end he just looked me in the eye and said, "That's right."

Annoyed by his glibness, I probed further. What was right? Was this the way everyone's inner world worked? "There is no inner and outer. It is all the same thing," he replied irritably. "Learn to see this." The subject was closed. The next thing I knew we were climbing into his car and driving across town to have breakfast at a fast food restaurant near the freeway on ramp.

Reflecting on the peyote experiences and my conversations with the spirit guides and other people who lived in my consciousness, it seemed to me that my spirit guides were emissaries between inner and outer worlds.

Over the next two or three years, I took peyote perhaps a dozen or more times. Thanks to the hallucinogens, I could carry on long conversations with the entities of my inner world, and even question what purpose this or that inner guide served in my life. On one occasion I even had a showdown with a character who had played tricks on me and manipulated me over the past years. Even while all this was occurring, I knew the difference between these ethereal manifestations and the *real* people in my life. At no time was I fearful that my communications with these entities were in any way pathological. This work seemed as natural and meaningful as anything I could imagine doing. Rather than fear or bewilderment, I finally experienced a great sense of relief, a feeling of *Aha! At last all the cards are on the table!*

To get to that point that I could consult with my inner guides without the stigma attached to this process during my childhood, I had to constantly struggle with my own doubts. Like so many people who had spirit guides, or imaginary playmates early in their lives, I had to overcome those early memories of humiliation and even parental concern. There's no doubt in my mind that what helped me move beyond this was a series of events that occurred around the time of my father's death, in 1973. It was at this time that I learned how the guides can help us in very direct and purposeful ways, giving us strength and knowledge to deal with some of life's greatest challenges. ~

Note: Peyote is a sacred medicine. I do not advocate its use except as such and only then with guidance of a shaman or psychotherapist who is experienced in its use and respects its powers.

A Glimpse of the Greater Reality

What is this greater reality? It views the mind as more than a brain compiling information like a mere computer. It views human consciousness as part of a greater reality in (and perhaps beyond) time and space, not as the epiphenomenon of an organism with a limited time span in the physical body.
--Brian O'Leary, Ph.D.
Exploring Inner and Outer Space

Undoubtedly one of the most dramatic uses of spirit guides, and one that confirmed my belief that they could be useful even at a practical level, came for me upon hearing that my father was dying. Dad was nearly 80 years old at the time and had lived a full and satisfying life. I am sure he was better prepared for his death than I or any of our other family members were.

I had no idea how to deal with his death. I got the news of his hospitalization over the phone, from 3,000 miles away, and immediately after that call I went to my office to make arrangements to fly back to Michigan to be with him in his last hours. As I sat in my study at home, I remembered that I had written down a dream I'd had of his death nearly two years before. Having done dream work for several years, I had a great number of journals to go through, but I was finally able to find the dream of my father's death and study what it said.

In the dream my father was lying in a hospital room. It was winter. There were two windows, one pointing east, one pointing north, and looking to the east I saw a huge harbor. There was a door leading from the north wall of this building down some wooden steps to a row of docks. In the dream my father died and I saw his spirit leave his body. I then led his spirit--which still had the shape of his body--to a strange looking boat, whose pilot, a man dressed like a fisherman and approximately my father's age, stood on the deck waiting for him.

My father and the boatman greeted each other in a friendly way, Dad a bit nervous but showing no fear or hesitation. He seemed to be anticipating the meeting with a certain amount of excitement. The boatman and he shook hands, and then the two of them stood back for a few moments to admire the boat, which had beautifully finished teak decks. My father, who had been a furniture maker much of his life, had an eye for fine finishes and he was quite impressed with the workmanship of this boat.

At last the boatman told my father that it was time

to go. Dad turned to me and to my surprise asked my permission to leave, which I gave him. He then went over a checklist he'd made up concerning each family member, asking me to confirm that they were all doing okay. It seemed that he did not feel good about leaving before he received this confirmation. I reassured him everyone was doing well, and I was certain they all gave him permission to leave us. He asked me to say goodbye to them for him, and I promised him that I would. Then he and I embraced, kissed, and he got into the boat. The dream ended with my standing on the dock watching the boat disappear out over the horizon.

I read the dream and wept. Besides being a dream of my father's death, it was a reminder of how estranged I'd become from him over the past twenty years, and now there would be little opportunity to make up for it. Sadder still, I hadn't the vaguest idea what had caused the distance between us, so even if we were given the chance to mend whatever differences we had, I wouldn't know where to start.

At this time in my life I had tentatively begun communicating with Alex again. Surprisingly, I found that he had aged, just as human beings do. He was no longer the teenaged boy I remembered from my childhood but was now a man approaching middle age. I had no sooner turned my thoughts to Alex than he instantly appeared in my mind's eye. When I told him about my father dying he said very quietly that I should go and be with him, and that I was to be his guide to the other side. I was appalled by the suggestion. I argued with Alex that I knew nothing about such things, that I had never been with anyone dying and wouldn't be able to handle it.

Alex told me not to worry, that it would be difficult but that I would get help along the way and the whole thing would go quite smoothly.

"Exactly how will I get this help?" I asked.

"Oh, you know," he said, mockingly. "You meet somebody, you tell them what you need and you ask a question."

He said all this flippantly, implying that this was so obvious and elementary that I should never have asked. I nevertheless pressed him to give me a sign, to tell me what I should be seeking in my helpers.

At this point he began to poke fun at me. He hunched up his shoulders, screwed up his face and in a rather humorous way, as if satirizing himself, he spoke in a voice reminiscent of Bela Lagosi playing Dracula.

He said, "*Zee* first person you meet will be an older *voman*. Let her know where you are going and why. Then go with her and she *vill* tell you very important information!"

I did not at all like his clowning around at a time like this. I was quite put off by it, thinking it in poor taste to be making jokes about such a serious situation.

His only response was to shrug off my criticism, as if to say, "Have it your way. It makes no difference to me."

An hour or so later I went down to the travel agency to pick up my plane ticket for the trip back to Michigan. Then, on the way out the door I literally bumped into an older woman! I excused myself and backed away from her, with the intention of moving on. Then I recognized her as the real estate saleswoman from whom I'd purchased our house several years before.

"Ah, Hal Bennett," she said, "Are you taking a trip?"

The instant she spoke I remembered her thick accent, left over from her childhood in Southern Italy, indeed, the region of the Dracula stories that my spirit guide had mimicked only an hour before. Stunned, I remembered Alex' advice about how I would meet an older woman who would assist me. This was too much of a coincidence! Was it possible that Alex really had known this woman would appear?

Somewhat shakily, I told the woman that my father was dying and I was going back to Michigan to be with him.

"Ah hah, yes!" Without a moment's hesitation she said, "You must come to my office right now. I have something very important to tell you."

"Right," I replied. Recalling my spirit guide's earlier admonishment, I realized that this was the "older woman" Alex had described, complete with the accent that I thought he had used to be sardonic. I had totally misjudged him.

The woman's office was only a few doors from the travel agency, and we went there immediately. She locked the outer door and invited me to sit down beside her desk. Then, like a teacher instructing a pupil she told me how less than a year before she had sat with her father as he was dying. It turned out he died from exactly the same disease that my father was suffering from.

Without my asking her a single question, the woman gave me a huge amount of information about the disease and what would happen, how Dad would become extremely agitated and restless, how he would hallucinate, and how I might comfort him. She also said that for her the experience of sitting with her father in his death had been "a great privilege, as wondrous as the birth of my children," and that even though she deeply mourned his loss, being present with her father in his death had enriched her life.

"This can be a great gift to you and to him," she said of my own situation. "You must open your heart and your mind to it completely."

I told her how grateful I was for her help. We hugged, and I promised that I'd report back to her as soon as I returned from my trip.

On the airplane to Detroit I closed my eyes and pictured Alex clearly in my mind. I thanked him for encouraging me to listen to the older woman. That moment in the travel agency, and later in the realtor's office, convinced me that I should stay open and trust that the kind of help I needed would be provided. Alex confirmed this, telling me that I would continue to get all the assistance I required. He added that I should look upon the dream I'd had as a guiding dream, a map for what I must do.

My brothers met me at the airport in Detroit, and that evening I went to the hospital. The man I saw in the bed bore only a vague resemblance to the mental image that I had of my father. His lips were parched and bleeding, and he was badly dehydrated despite an iv feeding fluids into his failing body.

Dad was happy to see me. He asked about my trip from California, and asked about his grandchildren. We made small talk, and from time to time he dozed off. In the beginning he was peaceful and outgoing, though his strength was obviously failing.

As that day passed, then another and another, my father's mood changed. He became agitated and impatient with the medical staff, didn't want them in his room. He asked to have the IV removed from his arm, which I did for him, and then he began refusing any further medication. In the last couple days of his life no-one but family members entered his room. We dismissed the medical staff and they happily made themselves scarce. It was clear that they did not like dealing with death.

As he severed himself more and more from the medical support system, Dad's dependence on us grew. I seemed able to calm him when he panicked, when he thrashed about on the bed, complaining of pain or his loss of bowel control. It was Alex who helped me at these moments, explaining that all I needed to do was to place my hand lightly over my father's heart and stay in a peaceful place in my own mind by meditating. My father's body was no longer important; I had to address my attention to his spirit. This I did, and I was amazed at how well it went, calming him even more effectively than the hospital's pain drugs had done before he refused to take them any more.

Toward the second or third day he had begun hallucinating heavily, just as my friend the real estate woman had told me he would. The contents of these hallucinations were very meaningful, and very private.

When I sought Alex' help with Dad's hallucinations and visions, he told me, "Let your father have these illusions. Do whatever you can to confirm his reality, whatever that reality might be to him. The hallucinations are all he has at this moment. Don't argue with him or try to convince him they aren't real, because to him they are real. If he seems frightened about them, ask him what you can do to help, and then do it, though it may require you to act in a world that you cannot see. Just keep in mind that there are many realities that cannot be confirmed by our five senses, and that is where you can be of the greatest service to your father now."

Following these instructions I spent a good part of one day and most of another miming out little rituals such as straightening up a bookshelf that wasn't there, or scratching the toes of my father's left leg--which had been amputated many years before. Some of these rituals were on the order of daily housekeeping, some went much deeper than that, communicating with people whose presence I could not see but who were playing out important dramas in Dad's life.

One of the most disturbing things to me was a recurring image when I sat beside my father with my hand on his heart. He would grow peaceful, almost blissful. Then an image would come into my mind of him and me in an invisible vehicle of some sort, racing out over a desert. My father appeared to be enjoying this--but I wasn't. The speed picked up, and the faster we went the more nervous I became. Finally, I would jump, startled, and at that point I would leave my meditative space and my father would become increasingly agitated.

This experience happened several times. One afternoon my younger brother Paul came to relieve me, and I drove back to my mother's house to rest. On the way back I asked Alex what the ride in the invisible vehicle represented. He told me that it was Dad's image of his passage from life to death, and I had nothing to fear from it. I asked if this meant that my dream about the passage taking place in a boat had been wrong. Alex said no, it was not wrong, but everyone had his own image to symbolize his passage, and the boat was mine. The passage would be the same, he said, regardless of the vehicle involved.

I asked Alex what I should do about the startle reflex because I did not want to continue projecting my own fear to my father. Alex instructed me that I should go for a walk to a specific place I had often gone as a teenager. I was told exactly where to go, which was a cedar swamp at the edge of the lake where I'd grown up.

It was in the dead of winter, and I had to borrow hiking boots and warm clothes to get where I was going. Directed by Alex, I came to a clearing in the woods. There before me was a primitive structure I'd made as a child. I had cut and lashed together several saplings, forming a crude pyramid frame with a fallen tree at the center, upon which I'd often sat. As a teenager, I'd intended to build a little hut in this spot. I'd planned that the lashed-together saplings would be the framework for the roof. When I built them, twenty years before, I had no idea that they'd formed a pyramid.

Sitting within the pyramid, I turned toward the lake, closed my eyes, and began to meditate. A few minutes passed. Then I imagined that I saw a figure in a red hunting coat coming toward me. I sensed Alex' presence, too, and he was telling me to greet this person and talk to him.

As the figure in the red coat grew clearer in my mind, I realized that it was me, as a boy of 17. Though I was certain of this, I asked him to identify himself. "I am the boy who came back from the dead," he said. "Don't you remember?"

He reminded me that when I was fifteen or sixteen years old I had contracted rabbit fever from a sick animal I had killed for the dinner table, and that I had been in a coma for nearly two days as a result. I had stood at that proverbial junction between life and death, fully aware that the decision to live or die was completely up to me at that moment. I remember this experience very clearly, even to this day. There was no fear. Death seemed to pose no threat. And I could not understand how to make the decision between life and death. Whichever choice I made seemed arbitrary.

That night I hovered somewhere above my body, from a distance of fifty feet or more. My body lay in the bed, packed in ice, in an effort to bring my fever down. I watched as my father entered the hospital room and dragged a chair up beside my bed. He was crying and holding my flaccid hand. I could not figure out why he was crying. I knew that my own death was near but I could not, for the life of me, understand the reason for his grief. Now that I saw death clearly I saw nothing to fear and nothing to grieve.

I had never seen my father cry like this. It mystified me that there could be such a powerful link between my dying and his grief. And I now believe that it was my curiosity about this mysterious link, as well as deference to my father's tears, that caused me to choose life over death at that moment. Had he not come to sit with my body at that moment I am quite certain I would have chosen death.

So I had come back from the dead. The struggle back was not easy. I returned to a body that was emaciated and weak. The fever had burned away virtually every hair and I found that I was blind, able to see only vague outlines of light and shadow. Indeed, I had been able to see more when my spirit hovered above the bed, free of my disease-riddled body.

Now, twenty plus years later, I was recalling all of this. Alex, my spirit guide, was making certain that I saw it, that I recognized that I was here, in part, to serve my father as he had served me. Except that this time I was to help him choose death and cross over. But there I was, sitting under a pyramid of cedar saplings, lashed together nearly two decades before, contemplating a dream figure in a red hunting jacket.

I asked the Boy Who Came Back From The Dead what he would do to help me. He said he didn't know, but that he would stay with me and when the time came that he could help he would let me know.

The next day when I went back to visit my father at the hospital he was worse. Much of the time he lay very still, his eyes closed. When he did awaken for a second or two he seemed not to connect with anything going on in the room. He frequently called me by another name and when he did I answered him as though I was that person. If he asked me to take care of something that wasn't there I obeyed.

Most of the time I sat by his bed and meditated, as before, with one hand on his chest. The image of the invisible vehicle carrying the two of us out over the desert was always there now but the ride seemed slow and sane and I did not grow frightened.

Toward evening I became aware of my older brother coming into the room and just standing there, staring at my father. I was deep in meditation, and was concentrating on the image of the vehicle, hoping it wouldn't speed up and frighten me. I was clearly aware of the fact that the speed of the vehicle was gradually picking up and there was nothing I could do about it.

The vehicle's speed increased by the second, so I finally asked for help from my inner guide. Alex appeared, simply looked at me, and then shrugged. He did not know what to do except to advise me to ask for help from The Boy Who Came Back From The Dead. Instantly, The Boy Who Came Back From The Dead appeared, saying that he could take my place in the vehicle now. He did this, and I watched as my father and he raced off. At that moment I felt relieved of a great burden, and I felt grounded and at peace.

Early the next morning my father died. He went in the most peaceful way imaginable, drifting off to sleep, never to awaken. But not before my older brother and I hugged him, told him that we loved him, and said goodbye.

Months after Dad died, my older brother described what had been going through his mind that evening when he entered the hospital room and stood so still, staring at Dad and me. My brother told me that he saw what appeared to be an ethereal copy of Dad's body floating above the bed, connected to the navel of the physical body below it by a thin, organic-looking thread. Nearly a year later my brother discovered, quite by chance, that yogis report that this is a common experience of people who are close to a dying person, and that it represented the spirit leaving the physical body.

Throughout those days of my father's dying, and even for weeks afterward, Alex continued to serve me. He maintained a calm presence, even during some of the most horrible and disconcerting, for me, moments. With his calm presence, he was always a touch stone for me, a reminder that my fear and trembling were of my own making, that seen from the higher perspective that Alex knew, my fears were no more than vanity.

Where Is The Proof?

There is no way to objectively confirm these experiences. The only part that can be confirmed, even anecdotally, is that my inner guides, Alex and The Boy Who Came Back From The Dead, clearly served important functions that allowed me to be with my father in ways that were helpful to him, to me, and hopefully to the entire family. Had I not allowed myself to receive the help I got from these inner guides, the entire experience could have been repulsive and fearful. With their help we were able to be with Dad, to give him our love and our caring even through the last moments of his life.

We know from our anthropological studies of ancient peoples, and from our study of the practice of *channeling,* that when a person takes on the character of an animal, a goddess or god, or another person, they gain access to information that they don't have in their everyday lives. This practice is as old as story telling and the use of masks. Certainly, in the wearing of masks, something almost magical occurs. We change character. If we're willing, we become the character depicted by the mask.

There is a story told to me by a friend who lived for several years on the Zuni reservation, in New Mexico, where she was a grade school teacher. A single parent, she also brought up her own child there. One day, when my friend's daughter was seven years old, she was sitting on a wall watching the Katchina dancers as they paraded through town during Shalako, a traditional day of ceremony.

The Katchinas, the Zuni believe, are spirits who were once in human form. In their passage to the spirit world, they have evolved into higher beings who now return to Earth from time to time, to teach people certain spiritual principles.

During ceremonies, appointed people in the community don the masks of these spirits and through practice and ceremony they slowly assume the specific character of the Katchina. In many cases, the right to carry and act out a Katchina has been passed down in the same family, through many generations. This is considered a great privilege and is taken very seriously.

My friend's child, sitting on the wall, was watching these traditional dances when her Zuni friend, of about the same age, turned to her and whispered, "Do you know the secret of the Katchinas?" My friend's daughter replied, no, she did not. The Zuni girl then whispered in her ear, "There's real people in there!"

Here was a child who probably knew each of the people dancing the Katchinas. Next door neighbors, cousins, the man who worked behind the counter in the local convenience store...all of them were people she'd be familiar with in the tiny village of Zuni. But so thoroughly did they assume the characters of the Katchinas that there was nothing to betray their everyday identity. The fact is, whatever the mask and costume represented to the dancer, had the power to allow the dancer to dissolve his own ego and personality self and adopt the mannerisms and the wisdom of the spirit figure. Indeed, this practice is a transcendent experience for most of the dancers.

In workshops where people access their own spirit guides, there are always many surprises. We have seen people assume the character of, say, an eagle, and describe the experience of flight. We've seen young people become grandmothers or grandfathers, speaking like them, even looking like them, and bringing closure to family mysteries or grievances. In one case, a woman who'd been quite reticent during a four-day workshop took on the character of a very entertaining and wise crone. Dancing about in a halting, yet graceful swirl of movement, the crone cackled like a raven, then stopped in front of each person in the room to give a bit of advice and insight totally appropriate for that individual.

These are all examples of working with spirit guides. Either outwardly or within the quietude of your own consciousness, characters appear who clearly access information, as well as a way of being, that you were not aware that you knew. This can, of course, be explained in several different ways. Perhaps by dropping some of our ego boundaries, or assuming different ones, we are activating parts of our minds that we don't ordinarily access. Maybe the mind stores far more information than the everyday self is able or willing to allow into full consciousness. Somehow, by assuming different characters we switch channels and so become aware of areas of consciousness that were hidden away until then.

We know that when we write or read novels, we

enter the lives and the minds of people very unlike ourselves. And we learn from this, our view of the world is changed, our perceptions broadened. For a little while we enter the lives of the characters we're reading about, or we share the thoughts and feelings of the author. The writer's skills create a container that holds us in worlds very unlike our own, and in the process we transcend our own limits.

If the spirit guide can be explained in these terms, as little more than products of the imagination, it does not, however, diminish the impact of this process on our lives. The ability to assume different characters for the sake of momentarily transcending your everyday perceptions of the world can indeed be valuable. This consciousness tool can enrich your life in quite extraordinary ways.

When he was a young man, C.G. Jung wrote a small book titled The Seven Sermons to the Dead (*Septem Sermones ad Mortuos*). In that booklet he reported on characters, or spirit guides, who instructed him in a way of looking at the world that was quite different from his scientific training as a physician and psychoanalyst. Indeed, to read this early writing the person who knows Jung's writing well will find the seeds for many of his most progressive and creative ideas that he developed during his extraordinarily productive life.

When we look at work such as this, and at other so-called channeled quality works of people such as Jane Roberts (*Seth Speaks*) or Helen Schucman (*A Course in Miracles*), and we compare the knowledge and experience of the authors to the knowledge and experience of their spirit guides we often find significant disparities. The dissimilarities, or even contradictions between the two suggest that the authors really are tapping into a source of information very different from their own. There is no way of proving this, of course, but after studying some of these channeled works, one is inclined to agree with Jung in his assessment of his own spirit guide, Philemon:

Philemon and other figures of my fantasies brought home to me the crucial insight that there are things in the psyche which I do not produce, but which produce themselves and have their own life. Philemon represented a force which was not myself.

In his discussion of the role Philemon played in his intellectual and spiritual life, Jung said that his spirit guide "represented superior insight...a mysterious figure to me. At times he seemed to me quite real, as if he were a living personality."

Jung also speaks of meeting a friend of Gandhi's, a spiritual leader from India, who Jung described as a gentleman of considerable sophistication and education. At one point, Jung asked the man about his spiritual education and what guru he had studied with. The man replied, matter-of-factly, that it was Shankaracharya. Jung, who knew this teacher as a commentator on the Vedas, who had died centuries before, was astonished. When he asked for clarification, the man replied that his guru was indeed the same person.

Jung then asked him if he was referring to a spirit teacher.

The man replied that this was so and that there are many people who have spirits for teachers. For Jung, this was welcome confirmation for his own experiences with his early *Seven Sermons* as well as his later work with Philemon and other spirits.

Respect for an Ancient Tradition

In making use of his communications with spirit guides, Jung was actually working within a well-established tradition. For example, it is generally accepted that the Vedas, part of one of the oldest religious scriptures in the world, were based on revelations channeled by ancient Indian sages. In a similar way, according to Moslem faith, the Koran was channeled by Mohammed during long visionary states. In more modern times, the works of Alice Bailey were channeled to her by a spirit guide she identified only as *The Tibetan* Others we might add to this list include Pat Rodegast's *Emmanuel's Books*, Andrew Ramer's two books, *Angel Answers* and *Revelations For A New Millennium,* and David Spangler's *New Age Transformations: Revelations*, to name but a few.

In Gnostic thought, as well as in many Eastern religions and the spiritual teachings of several Native American peoples, the universe and everything we observe, is of one consciousness. Further, we are not at all separate from this consciousness but a part of it. In his *Seven Sermons*, Jung's spirit guide calls this consciousness the *pleroma*, and said of it: "We are the pleroma itself, for we are a part of the eternal and infinite."

As the pleroma itself, each and every one of us is capable of accessing anything that the pleroma embraces--which is everything. My own opinion is that were we to constantly be open to this infinite knowledge and infinite experience, we would probably go mad. To make it possible for us to function in our physical form, our brains, and in particular our personalities, or egos, act as filters, allowing us to keep our knowledge somewhat manageable.

When we access spirit guides, or even if we create them, we change those filters that our personalities provide. These different characters allow us to expand our own capacities and our own awareness, dipping into areas of the pleroma, with its infinite knowledge, that would otherwise never be accessible to us. I am reminded of the words of William James, one of the fathers of modern psychological research:

> *Most people live...in a very restricted circle of their potential being. They make use of a very small portion of their possible consciousness, and of their soul's resources in general, much like a man who, out of his whole bodily organism, should get into a habit of using and moving only his little finger.*

Through work with spirit guides, we begin to move into the intuitive and mystical realms, areas of human experience that we have gravely neglected in our zeal to measure, categorize and quantify the universe. Perhaps through our explorations of the intuitive realm, blending modern techniques with ones that are thousands of years old, we can become more familiar with our soul's resources and how they can enhance the quality of our lives.~

Lifelong Spirit Companions

If these processes point the way toward the existence of other intelligences, then we have access to domains that are probably beyond our imagination.
~Arthur Hastings, With the Tongues of Men and Angels

Throughout history we humans have sought ways to understand the invisible forces that govern our lives. By this I mean spiritual and emotional forces-- the soul's resources--whose presence we know not by what our five senses tell us but by what our hearts and souls tell us. We know them through feelings such as love and compassion; we know them when we gaze at the heavens at night, observing the order of the planets; we know them when we hold a newborn in our arms and contemplate the mystery of life itself. In early societies, humans donned masks and costumes that personified these forces—the goddess of love, the fertility goddess, the god of war, etc.—to acknowledge and honor them.

As the actor or dancer dressed up in costumes and masks, and followed the rhythms of drummers, musicians and other dancers, he or she was transformed, seemingly abandoning everyday ego concerns to the divine character of the god, goddess or spiritual force they were depicting. The actors suspended their personal concerns and focused their attention on universal truths which we all know intuitively, though we may or may not ever learn to articulate them. The mask, costume, rhythms and movements all around them focused the actors' attention on the force or character they represented, giving them permission to transcend the physical boundaries of their own lives and focus more intently, through their hearts and souls, so that they might express truths beyond verbal understanding.

In my twenties and early thirties, I worked in the theater, fascinated by the way people with acting skills, and with the help of a good script, could access qualities and understandings they did not appear to otherwise have. The person who was meek and withdrawn offstage could become a convincing despot when he assumed a tyrannical character on stage. The woman whose life was a complete mess offstage became a noble leader on stage. I am convinced these transformations didn't happen only because the actor was being given the right words to say, or the dramatic setting to become a certain character. Surely that was part of it. More than this, actors appeared to go through a personal transformation. For that brief moment on the stage, he or she embodied strengths and virtues that inspired or horrified their audience, tapping into resources that at times seemed nothing short of miraculous.

Knowing dozens of actors, on and off the stage, I found it absolutely fascinating to ponder the puzzle of how far the human consciousness was able to stretch, how far beyond our everyday capacities we can reach under certain circumstances. Indeed, there were performances which absolutely convinced me that consciousness itself has no boundaries, or at least that it extends far beyond the confines of the bony box that holds our brains.

Out of my experiences in the theater, I became convinced that spirit guides start out as something akin to characters in a play. Then, as we give ourselves over to that character our individual personalities slip away and our consciousnesses are liberated, reaching into pools of awareness outside our everyday self. By assuming these characters, we create a way of experiencing a different reality.

In the summer of 1970, while visiting the home of my doctor friend, Michael Samuels, with whom I wrote several health books, we got into a discussion about spirit guides. I expressed my theory that they were something like sub-personalities that let us look at life in a slightly different way, thus giving us access to a different perspective and possibly a vast new storehouse of knowledge. I fully expected Dr. Samuels to agree with me. Since he was a medical doctor with a scientific background, I believed he would take a skeptical, scientific position on spirit guides.

We were sitting on the deck at his Marin County

home, enjoying a beautiful, clear day on the coast. In the distance, the ocean stretched out to the end of the earth, merging with a brilliant, blue sky. Down in Mike's apple orchard the trees were filled with fruit and a warm summer breeze carried their sweet fragrance. A hawk circled overhead. It was one of those idyllic days when there seemed to be all the time in the world to sit and talk.

Mike patiently listened to my theories about spirit guides. Then he said that a year ago he might have agreed with me, but since then he had several first hand experiences that made him ask some very different kinds of questions. Without arguing his case, he asked me if I had ever had an imaginary playmate as a child. I admitted I did indeed have one. In fact, I could remember him quite vividly.

Mike then told me that he had recently learned a way to get a spirit guide, and asked if I wanted to give it a try. We talked about it for awhile and he described what the process involved--mostly going into a deeply relaxed place in my mind and becoming receptive to meeting a guide. It sounded simple enough, so I told him I'd like to do it.

Sitting in the warm sun that bathed the countryside, Mike instructed me to close my eyes as he talked me through what seemed like a simple relaxation exercise. As I relaxed, I let myself be guided my Mike's voice, asking me to imagine that I was standing in front of a house. The house that came to my mind was a very old one, built in the Tudor style, with its heavy, plank door opening out onto the narrow, cobblestone street. It was my impression that I was in a European city and that the house I was seeing was perhaps several hundred years old. There were cars around, so it wasn't as if I'd gone far back in time, but the makes and models were not ones I was familiar with, and most seemed to be from the thirties.

I had never been to Europe so it seemed odd to me that all this would appear so real, like visiting a place where I'd previously spent a good deal of time. I heard a bell ringing, far in the distance, tolling the time, and somehow knew it was coming from a clock tower in a public square not far away. I heard voices of people passing by, and determined that they were speaking English, but with a thick British accent that I barely understood.

I commented on this to Mike and he told me not to talk but to stay focused on my imaginary journey. He told me to knock on the door of the house where I was standing. I did this. After a moment, I heard a lock being released inside. The door opened and a skinny young woman wearing a light green apron that covered the whole front of her body, greeted me. It was as if she had been expecting me. I did not know exactly what to say or do but this turned out to be unnecessary since she directed me up a wide staircase off to my right, and pointed to a door on the uppermost landing. I dutifully followed her instructions, assuming she knew more than I did.

At the assigned door, I knocked lightly. When nobody answered I went inside. It was empty except for a few straight-backed chairs, giving me the impression that this was a room which was never used. I reported what I saw to Mike and he suggested that I sit down in a chair and imagine seeing a door in front of me, through which my guide would come. The door was a special sliding door, opening at the bottom and slowly raising up so that I saw my spirit guide a little at a time. I sat down, as instructed. In a moment the door started opening, showing me the sturdy shoes of a woman with rather large legs. As the door inched upwards, I saw a white lab coat, a thick waist, and finally a complete person.

Disappointed that it was not the imaginary playmate from my childhood--and quite surprised that it wasn't--I nevertheless was curious and sat patiently, waiting to see what would happen next.

This new guide introduced herself to me as Dr. Hilda. She was a middle-aged, somewhat overweight medical researcher with a Germanic accent and a very stuffy manner. She wore no makeup, her cheeks fleshy and plain, with jowls that made her face quite round. She had short, close-cropped, graying hair, and her starched, white, oversized lab coat made it impossible to get much of a sense of her body.

She was quite amiable, in spite of her stern appearance, and cordially offered to show me what she called her laboratory. I got up and followed her into a room with a lot of stainless steel and glass cases and tables. I asked Dr. Hilda what she was doing in my life, and she replied that she was here to teach me about some healing work she had been observing.

She told me to stand in a particular place in her

laboratory, which I did. She took her place beside me and in an instant we were transported to an entirely different setting. We were now in a jungle, a dense, steaming atmosphere of very tall trees. I stood in a grove of ferns that towered over my head. Hilda put her finger to her lips, warning me to keep silent, then pointed to a clearing just beyond a border of green. I heard a man softly chanting, his voice deep and resonant, the rhythms blending with the sounds of nature all around us. I asked Dr. Hilda what this was all about.

"It is a healing ritual," she said.

I peered into the clearing, careful to keep myself hidden behind the wall of ferns and broad-leafed plants. In the center of the clearing I saw two figures. The first was a very old and very wizened black man, sitting on the ground in a semi-lotus position, his head bowed and his eyes closed. He was naked except for something in his hair, which turned out to be leaves, or clumps of fresh herbs.

A second black man, this one younger and dressed in a white loincloth, danced around him. His movements were simple, rhythmic, and repetitive, barely varying as he circled the man on the ground again and again. He chanted as he moved, his voice deep, resonant, and soothing.

"What are they doing?" I asked Dr. Hilda.

"The man on the ground is dying, the other is a holy man, what you would call a medicine man. His name is Ubanga, or Uvani. Different people call him by different names. I believe one name is his common name, the other is what you call him when he is doing his work."

"Does he know you're studying him?"

"Yes, of course," Dr. Hilda said. "In this work, you do not observe without permission."

"And the holy man. What exactly is the medicine he is using?"

"Rhythm. His medicine is in the rhythms of his chanting and movements."

"Does it work?" I asked. I must admit that I was more than a little skeptical. I could not see how movement and rhythm could possibly heal anyone or why a medical researcher of Dr. Hilda's apparent status would think it a legitimate subject for serious research.

Dr. Hilda smiled. "Yes," she insisted. "Uvani is a great healer, and his dance is great medicine."

"What is the disease he is healing?"

"The fear of death. He is working with the man's resistance to death. Uvani is helping him make the passage. He knows the way because he has been there himself. In his youth he died after being bitten by a poisonous snake. But he came back from the land of death and now he helps others make this passage."

Let me note here that this occurred at least a year before my father's death and I believe was to be an important source of strength for me when I was called to his bedside. At the time of my introduction to Hilda and this bizarre jungle scene, I did not see how helping someone die could be called healing. To me, healing was outwitting death, not cooperating with it.

We stayed at the edge of the clearing for only a few moments, then Dr. Hilda said it was time to go back. Instantly, we were transported back to her sterile laboratory, with its white walls, stainless steel and spotless glass, a shocking contrast to the jungle setting where we'd watched Uvani.

Moments later, I shifted my focus again and was back on Dr. Samuel's deck, bathed in warm sunlight. As I opened my eyes and looked around, however, nothing seemed familiar to me. This is difficult to describe. Although I knew exactly where I was, the world seemed fresh to me, as if I was seeing it for the first time. Coming from the imaginal world I'd just visited, and popping so suddenly back into my everyday life, I now felt as if everything around me was a fantasy. Reality had become story-book magic, where colors were too brilliant, and the depth of the landscape exaggerated, like viewing the first 3-D films with special glasses. Smells were intense, and I became particularly aware of the scent of the eucalyptus trees and blossoming fruit trees all around the Samuels' property.

I continued to experiment with this spirit guide process, and in the fall of the following year I received another guide. This one came through in a dream. It is worth noting here that this is not at all unusual. You might, for instance, do the exercise for getting a guide and receive nothing at the time. But that night, or even several nights later a figure comes through in a dream, whose presence is so vivid and clear that you cannot ignore them. In any case, this is what happened for me.

This guide introduced himself to me as the spirit of a famous person who had been dead for nearly twenty years. He had been a writer, and I was somewhat familiar with his work. I knew him as a man who in real life had experimented with the occult. So it was natural that I would have gravitated toward his writing. Though I had never known him in real life, I admired him and felt I knew him, in many ways, as one might know a well-rendered character from a favorite novel.

I saw him as tall and slender, with thinning gray hair and piercing blue eyes so bright and lively they defy his age. He is more than a little clumsy in his movements, reminding me of a teenager who has not quite grown into his body. I usually picture him wearing a tweed sports jacket, a sports shirt open at the collar, and light tan dress pants. He always has a rumpled look about him, his outward appearance never having been high on his priority list, even during his physical life.

Not long after making contact with this entity, I learned that his widow was living in the United States, and with a little detective work on my part was able to contact her. Being curious to know if she had ever had any contact with him since his death, and wanting to see if I could corroborate some things about him, I sent her a book I had written, with a little note asking if I could either meet with her or talk with her on the phone.

A month or two later, she called me and we spoke about her husband's interest in what she called "spiritism." She shared stories about his experiences with spirit guides, and we exchanged our own theories, and beliefs about such phenomena. She admitted that she was not as much of a believer as her husband had been. She had never experienced talking with spirits herself but said that she had always tried to keep an open mind about it. As the conversation drew to a close, she asked if I would be writing about these experiences, and I replied that I hadn't planned on it. But being a writer it was certainly a possibility. She then asked that if I did so, would I please not name her husband as my guide. I promised that I would keep his name a secret, a promise I've kept to this day. I said that if I did talk about him I would refer to him by the name of my childhood guide, Alex. Only this one would be known as Alex II. For all I knew, the two might be merged spirits or total fantasies on my part. I liked the idea that maybe this new guide was a grown up version of the earlier one.

When I later told this guide of my conversation with his wife, and said that I was going to be calling him Alex II from now on, he found all this quite amusing. He laughed and said that in spite of the fact that he did not picture himself as an Alex, it was quite all right if I called him that. After all, he said, in the spirit world there is very little need for names or any other of the trappings associated with the physical world. But as a person still embodied, I would not be satisfied unless I could picture my guides with names and physical bodies and clothing.

From the start, Alex helped me with my writing. When I wanted to get feedback about something I'd written, I had only to imagine him sitting across the desk from me and he would be there. He seemed to respect what I was doing, though he also seemed amused by it, in a nice way, I must add. He had clearly moved beyond the subjects which interested me but never gave even a hint of being critical or condescending. Alex was, and is, a gentle, kind entity, in spite of having an incredibly broad range of knowledge, on virtually every subject.

Within a few weeks of meeting Alex, I became quite accustomed to his presence, and stopped thinking of my association with him as anything unusual. I do remember, however, asking him to tell me about spirit guides. What are they? Do they really exist or do we fabricate them in our minds? Do they have autonomy, that is, do they operate separate from, or outside, our own consciousness?

Alex said that spirit guides exist in our consciousnesses as the result of the same human faculty that allows us to dream. But what, in fact, does it mean to dream? he probed. He told me not to take dreaming for granted, that it was something very different than we assumed it to be in modern life. He said the easiest way to think about dreaming was to consider that our dream world--our sleeping dreams as well as the state we enter when working with spirit guides--is a parallel reality, existing side by side with consensus reality. It is not a "made-up" or "pretend" reality, but one that in fact determines the course of everyday reality. Were it not for this invisible reality, he said, there could be no physical reality. The invisible reality, he insisted, is our foundation.

Alex insisted that there exists an aspect of human consciousness that makes it possible to experience and understand things that are not available to us in the usual ways, such as reading, attending lectures, watching an informative television program, or living through a significant event. There are ways to access wisdom and experience things other than through our physical senses, or even our brains.

While all this was intriguing to me, I found myself looking for some objective evidence that all this had any relationship to my everyday life. I still could find no valid argument repudiating my original theory that channeling was primarily a creative process.

Then one afternoon, I became very sleepy. I crossed my arms, put my head down on my desk and slipped off into a restless somnolence. I was aware of Alex' presence, but this was not unusual since he was frequently there whenever I was writing. As I drifted off, I imagined myself transported to a rugged seaside setting. There was a high cliff at the edge of the ocean, and I was walking along a trail at the top. It was windy and cold and I shivered under a yellow slicker someone had given me for this walk. Far below me, the waves crashed over rocks, sending huge geysers of spray thirty and forty feet into the air. I believe it was the area around Big Sur, California, just south of Carmel.

"There are twenty principles in all," Alex was saying.

"Principles?" I asked, feeling disoriented, as if I'd just tuned in to the middle of a television program and had no idea what was going on. "What principles are you talking about?"

Alex ignored my questions and went on talking, lecturing me about these twenty principles. When I awoke, I remembered only little pieces of the dream-- the walk along the spectacular coastline, the mention of the twenty principles, and my question about the number. Frankly, I was quite curious. The number twenty somehow seemed important, even though Alex had acted as if it wasn't. But what were the principles he was talking about? My memory of them consisted mostly of impressions.

Over the next few days, I entered into a long series of dialogues with Alex. Again he described the twenty principles to me, this time not in a dream but in waking dialogues that I recorded in my journals. I took the role of the student sitting at the master's feet. At other times, he took me on inner journeys to demonstrate the principles, as if the telling itself was not enough.

Today, I can honestly say that the twenty principles have become key guidelines in my own life. Whenever I turn to them, for help in my own life, I find them extremely helpful. Alex described these twenty principles as universal guidelines that exist for all people. They are, he said, as ancient as humanity itself, and will endure as long as the universe itself endures.

"Certain things," he told me, "become necessary when spirit, which is infinite, takes on a finite form, as it does when we are born into a physical body. Given brains, personalities and bodies, we appear to be separate and autonomous beings. In that form, we try to make sense of everything. We are limited, however, to making sense with our brains, forgetting what we truly are, forgetting that it is impossible to separate ourselves from the earth, from each other, from our friends or enemies, since all, everything, is nothing more than a thought."

"Whose thought?" I asked.

"Can't be answered."

"Can't be or you won't?"

"Can't be! Your mind, mistakenly believing itself to be a model of all Creation, imagines questions which quite simply don't exist, and certainly aren't relevant. And that's the crux of the whole problem."

"Which problem?" I asked.

Alex laughed. "I think we call it the human condition. The twenty principles I gave you become necessary only as rough guidelines for help with the human condition. But I warn you, they are not truths. They are only guidelines, necessitated by the peculiar circumstances you've come into by taking on this physical form. Truth always exists outside any of the faculties connected with that form, so this is the best we can do. Live these principles as if they were true, but never insist that they are. What you learn from them will either serve you well or not at all. Use them only as long as they serve."

(For the record, I used the twenty principles Alex dictated to me in a book titled *Mind Jogger*, which is published by Celestial Arts. It is available through any bookstore, or through my website, listed in the back of this book.)

I tell this story to illustrate some of the ways we can work with our guides and learn from them. But more than this, I'd like to make it clear that there are guides with whom we might maintain life-long relationships. It has been that way with Alex. I like to believe that the same spirit guide I have today is somehow linked with the much younger spirit guide from my childhood. I have asked but Alex' answers are more enigmatic than definitive. There's the implication that it is one of those questions that my brain likes to make up, but which is really of no relevance.

What I can say for certain is that there appears to be a continuity between the earlier guide and Alex. He knows what went before and having that continuity with him is important to me.

I consider Alex a teacher and counselor and his presence in my life--whether imagined or real--is a source of both comfort and edification. He is, in a very real way, a bridge to that invisible reality to which all of us are bound. And he is a friend, one who knows my life well--perhaps better than I know it!

As I approach the end of this chapter I am reminded of a quote by Holger Kalweit, from his remarkable book on shamanism, *Dreamtime and Inner Space* (Shambala Publications, 1988). In that book, he describes the experiences of a person who has entered and returned from that invisible reality that we've come to know, at least a little bit, through our spirit guides:

One person who returned said: 'It seemed that all of a sudden, all knowledge--of all that had started from the very beginning, that would go on without end--that for a second I knew all the secrets of the ages, all the meaning of the universe, the stars, the moon--everything.

Based on my own experiences with spirit guides, I have become convinced of at least two things: first, that there is a reality beyond that which we perceive through our five senses; and, second, that spirit guides can provide us with glimpses into the reality beyond our physical one, which like a nagging child demands so much of our attention. By establishing a practice of consulting with your guide(s) on a daily basis, this process becomes increasingly useful. And out of it comes a broader understanding of the invisible reality-- that which is the basis of all life.

Going Forward

In the following chapter, you'll find instructions for getting a personal spirit guide. Read these over before you actually sit down to do them. Then go forward, knowing that literally thousands of people have used these instructions successfully, opening their hearts and their minds to a wonderful source of information and assistance.

If you are presently working with a psychotherapist or psychologist, I recommend that you talk over the spirit guide exercise with her or him before you do it. Share this book with them. If they feel that this inner work might interfere with your psychotherapy, consider that possibility carefully before going on.~

Meeting Your Spirit Guides

Our physical boundaries may be much more illusory than real. Like the proverbial mirage of a cool, bubbling spring seen by the thirsty desert traveler, the boundaries we perceive between ourselves and the rest of the universe may best be understood as products of our minds.
~Stanislav Grof, M.D., with Hal Zina Bennett,
The Holotropic Mind

Upon entering this territory associated with spirit guides, it is natural to do so with a certain degree of caution, or even apprehension. Our apprehension grows from a realization that we are moving into the unknown. And our caution comes from recognizing that we are pioneering uncharted terrain. To enter any new territory is to risk changes in our outer life as well as our inner one. People who have not had much experience working with the inner world, or the world we associate with transcendental or transpersonal realms, will undoubtedly find their world views challenged.

The human mind, however, is very self-protective. When it detects that we are "getting in over our heads," it always puts out warning signals, in the form of fear, doubt, and that little voice within that says, "This is stupid, a farce. Why am I bothering with stuff that common, everyday reason tells me is sheer nonsense!"

It is important to pay attention to these signals. Ask what's behind them. For example, maybe these warnings are telling you that diving into this realm is going to challenge important relationships in your life. Is there a loved one who fears what you are doing, or who finds such beliefs distasteful? Are there important religious, or even scientific beliefs that you hold that would be challenged if you discovered that this other reality was valid and useful?

If you wish to go forward with your exploration of spirit guides, first try to answer some of these basic questions: What's behind your resistance or fear? What would you have to change in your relationships, or in your own professional beliefs, or in your world view? Don't take these questions too lightly. Give them the respect they deserve but also recognize that you have options other than simply responding to the fear or resistance by backing away from the experience entirely.

The options are to question what your resistance, doubts and fears are about and then make a conscious decision about whether to go forward or not. The novelist Andre Gide once said, "Don't understand me too quickly." This is always good advice where messages from our self-protective mechanisms are concerned. And it is the only way to move beyond our own prejudices, arrogance and superstitions.

The exercise you'll find here for meeting your spirit guide begins with deep relaxation. In a deeply relaxed state your mind slows and the visual cortex of your brain becomes more receptive and active. It is here, in the visual cortex, that the action of the spirit guide will first take place.

Much has been made, in recent years, of the importance of deep relaxation for exercises such as this. It is the kind of relaxation exercise that leads to the meditative state. In the meditative state, our brain waves are altered; we grow relaxed, so relaxed that we let go of the tensions and worries of the day and soon our minds go blank, or nearly blank. In this state, we enjoy the feeling of having nothing to think about or act upon. For a moment we truly cut ourselves off from the cares of the world.

This deeply relaxed state is easily achieved with the following exercise, though it may take repeated practice (from three to six or more tries) before you feel you can achieve the deep state of relaxation at will.

Letting Go of Preconceptions

If you have never done a deep relaxation or meditation exercise before, the scenario will probably go something like this: You'll scan the written exercise, which will seem simple enough, almost too simple to be taken seriously. Then you'll decide to give it a try.

As you begin to relax, something comes to mind that you feel simply must get done before you go on. Or, you begin going over events of the day in your mind. Or you begin to worry about something that at that moment you can't possibly do anything about anyway. And everything that comes to mind really is important.

Let yourself fully acknowledge the thoughts and feelings running through your mind. But tell yourself firmly, I do not have to act on any of these issues right now. It is perfectly all right to take ten or fifteen minutes for relaxing.

The issues, like spoiled children, may continue to try to compete for your attention. Here's what to do if that happens:

Stop and make a conscious decision. Ask yourself, should I stop relaxing, get up and do what I feel I must do, or should I let it go? If you really feel you need to take care of something, do it. You can come back to relax when you are done. Your decision to stop your meditation and do something else is as important to the process of learning deep relaxation as is a fifteen minute session with no interruptions.

Final Tips On Doing This Exercise

For best results you may wish to do this exercise with a friend, having them read it to you as you follow the directions to relax. You might also wish to make a cassette tape of it on your recorder and play it back to yourself. If you do this, read the exercise into the recorder in a monotone. Read slowly enough so that you can complete each step of the exercise before going onto the next one. It may take some trial and error before you get the right speed and pacing for the tape, but keep at it until you can sit back, play the tape, and go into a deeply meditative state by listening to your own voice.

The alternative is to record your voice as you read the exercise to a friend. Watch your friend's responses as you read, slowing down or speeding up when you encounter obstacles or your friend has a difficult time following you or letting their body do the exercise. An effective tape of this exercise will be paced to match the rate at which you are able to respond to at a deep, muscular level to each of the instructions.

Some people prefer to just read the exercise a few times so that they can sit back, relax and simply recall each step, thus moving easily through the instructions at their own pace.

Choose whichever process works best for you.

Part One: The Relaxation Exercise

Make a conscious decision to take five or ten minutes to relax. Give yourself permission to use your time in this way. Choose a time of day and a place to work where you will be free of distractions.

~Sit in an alert, upright position, your hands laying gently, palms open, on the tops of your legs.

~Let your shoulders be loose and relaxed.

~Relax your toes and let the entire soles of your feet make contact with the floor.

~Loosen any tight-fitting clothing.

~Open your mouth and yawn, or pretend you are yawning.

~Let the areas around your eyes be relaxed. Let your forehead be loose. Let the area around your nose and mouth be relaxed.

~If ideas or feelings urge you to think or act at this time, pretend they are a ringing telephone in another room. You may observe the sound of the "ringing," but don't feel that you must answer. Simply focus your attention on the quality of the bell's sound and remind yourself that truly important thoughts or feelings will return, if you wish them to, after you have finished relaxing.

~Take a deep breath. Hold it for a moment. Slowly exhale through your nose.

~Be aware of your chest relaxing.

~Take a deep breath. Hold it for a moment. Slowly

exhale through your nose.

~Be aware of your shoulders relaxing.

~Take a deep breath. Hold it for a moment. Slowly exhale through your nose.

~Be aware of your abdomen relaxing.

~Take a deep breath. Hold it for a moment. Slowly exhale through your nose.

~Be aware of your back and buttocks relaxing.

~Take a deep breath. Hold it for a moment. Slowly exhale through your nose.

~Be aware of your legs relaxing.

~Take a deep breath. Hold it for a moment. Slowly exhale through your nose. Feel the bottom of your feet where they make contact with the floor.

~Be aware of your feet relaxing.

~Now allow your breathing to return to normal. Enjoy this relaxed state.

~Just allow yourself to be in this relaxed state for a moment before you go on.

Part Two: Meeting Your Guide

While in a deeply relaxed state, do the following to meet your inner guide:

Imagine that you are out for a walk.

You may be walking in a city. Or in a small

village. Or in a woods. Or alongside a stream. Or near a lake or other large body of water. You may be in the mountains or by the ocean.

You feel safe. You feel confident. You are physically comfortable and at ease.

For a moment, just enjoy your walk.

You now approach a structure: it may be a small house, a large building, a rustic structure, a modern one. Stop for a moment and simply look at this structure.

Notice its size and style. Notice the area around it-- other houses, open fields, etc.

You now go up to the structure. You are standing at its entrance. You knock on the door or in some other way announce your presence.

You hear a voice in your mind, or you get some sort of signal to enter and go inside. You do this, feeling confident, safe and comfortable.

Step inside. Close the door behind you.

Look around you. Take note of what you see: the color of the walls and floors, whether the rooms are bright or dark, the furnishings you see, any nick-knacks that come to your attention.

Somewhere in this house you will meet your guide. This meeting may occur in the room where you are now standing. It may occur somewhere else. You will know exactly where you should be for this meeting. Go to that place now.

Imagine that you are now sitting down in the room where the meeting will take place. You are facing a special door. It is a sliding door that will open from the bottom up.

Your guide is now standing behind the door, waiting to meet you.

The door slides up a foot or so, then stops.

You see your guides feet. Take your time, now. Note what the guide is wearing: shoes and socks? what colors and styles? Or is your guide barefoot?

The door slides open a little more until you are able to see everything up to their waist. Note what they are wearing. You may also see their hands at this time, if they are standing with their hands at their sides. Note any jewelry they might be wearing.

The door now slides up as far as their neck. Again, note their clothes, if any, their posture, their size. Note any unusual personal items--a scarf, necktie or kerchief, necklace, broach, items in their pockets, etc.

Now the door fully opens and you see your guide's face for the first time. Take as close a look as you like. Look at their hair. Look at their forehead. Look at their eyes. Look at their mouth and chin. Look at their ears. Look at their neck.

If is time to greet your guide. In your mind, or out loud if you wish, say "Hello, my name is _____. I understand that you are my inner guide. I'd like to know your name."

Your guide steps forward now and greets you.

You may have a sense of them shaking your hand, or hugging you, or kissing you.

If you do not get a response right away, wait until you do get a response. This may come as a voice, clear and distinct like someone talking in the room where you are sitting, or it may come as a name that suddenly pops into your mind.

Imagine, now, that you and your inner guide sit down together and begin conversing. Talk on any subject, but in the first meeting limit yourself to a few minutes exchange.

When you feel like stopping, simply tell your inner guide that you wish to do so. Tell them that you are glad you met them and that you will come back to be with them, and converse with them another time. Shake hands, or in some other way bring a cordial closure to the meeting.

Now leave the room where you met and go to the front door of the building. Go outside.

When you are ready, take a deep breath. Open your eyes if they were closed. Yawn. Stretch. Slowly get up and walk around.

After You Have Met Your Inner Guide

After meeting your inner guide, give some thought to the meeting. Did it go as you wished? Did this guide seem to be someone you would like to meet and talk with in the future? If not, recognize at this point that you need not see them again. You can go back at a later date, do the exercise again, and get another guide.

If you are not certain you want to keep your guide, give yourself some time to think about it. There is no rush. And always remember, where your inner world is concerned you are the master. You may find things that surprise you but you can take control any time you wish.

If you didn't get an inner guide your first time around, don't worry. You can try again. Or, your guide may appear quite unexpectedly to you in the next day or two. The guide may even appear in a dream.

C.G. Jung reports that his first efforts to make contact with his inner guides were not without misgivings. At the time of his first experiments there was scant literature available on the subject of getting guides and working with them. He did not know if he could enter his inner world without "becoming a prey of the fantasies," and only after many years of exploring this inner world--both his own and his patients'--was he convinced that it was a safe territory to enter. The following describes his first experience of entering that world:

> *Then I let myself drop. Suddenly it was as though the ground literally gave way beneath my feet, and I plunged down into dark depths. I could not fend off a feeling of panic. But then, abruptly, at not too great a depth, I landed on my feet in a soft, sticky mass. I felt great relief, although I was in complete darkness. After a while my eyes grew accustomed to the gloom, which was rather like a deep twilight. Before me was the entrance to a*

dark cave, in which stood a dwarf with a leathery skin, as if he were mummified.

Over the years, Jung entered this territory time and time again, and for nearly a decade explored and got to know the various figures he met there. He reports that he learned much from his journeys, especially from the inner guide he would call Philemon.

Most of the time people are happy with the guides they get. Let's assume that you will be, too. In the days ahead, take every chance you can find to think about your guide, just as you might do after meeting a new friend. In the process of doing this their presence may become quite vivid for you. I don't mean that you will see them appear in the chair across the table or beside you as you stand in line at the supermarket. But you may feel their presence in much the way you do when thinking about a close friend. Take advantage of this moment to share any thoughts you might be having with your guide. You needn't talk aloud to them. Doing it in your mind is just fine.

Conversations with your guide need not always be on serious issues. You may pass the time of day with them. You may even share stories or jokes. It is not at all unusual to build up trust in your guide slowly, making small talk, getting to know them one step at a time, before entrusting this new relationship with a problem that is important to you.

Are Inner Guides Infallible?

Like people with physical bodies, the spirit guides can provide knowledge, comfort, counsel--in short, nearly all the qualitites that we seek in our everyday human relations. And just as in other relationships the guides can be the source of conflict, frustration, and anger.

The same things are true of spirit guides as are true of the people in our outer worlds. The illusions they are capable of weaving are no different than the illusions we weave for ourselves, or which we allow those we love to weave with us. We must see the spirit guides as being just as fallible as other humans in our lives.

Regardless of what they might tell you to the contrary, always remember that your spirit guides are, after all, only human. ~

Making Peace with Inner Critics

Did you know that the more we resist something, the more we're likely to be stuck with it? When we resist something, we project psychic energy to keep it away... Two opposing forces or energies come to a deadlock... In this way, we literally attract what we resist!
~ *Linda Keen,* Intuition Magic

Occasionally, people working with spirit guides will receive an entity that is quite the opposite of what they are seeking. It might make its appearance as nothing more than a nagging doubt, the kind of doubt or skepticism that you associate with everyday judgments about making a purchase or signing up for a new service. But these doubts may grow in strength until any hopes you had of getting and working with a spirit guide are undermined.

Your skepticism or doubt may take other forms as well. For example, you might have vivid recollections of a person from your childhood who was hypercritical of you or someone who was always warning you to be careful, to "color within the lines," to always follow the rules, or to adopt their way of thinking. Maybe this critical being was a person who was always comparing you to others, telling how you could do better and "achieve your potential" if you would only make a greater effort.

All these critical messages have the effect of inhibiting whatever you are doing or thinking at the moment, and in some cases they will stop you in your tracks. At the very least they prevent you from getting in touch with your own creative and intuitive abilities. While these are, on one hand, powerful capacities, they are also fragile, particularly when we are just beginning to discover them. Remember that we are living at a time in history when science and technology have become core concepts and anything that isn't easy to confirm within these thought systems is suspect. You're going to have to be willing to take a step beyond consensual reality if you wish to develop your intuitive and creative sides.

The knotty expressions of criticism and doubt that I describe here are all "inner critics," and I have never met a single person who didn't have at least one. They are different from spirit guides in that they are usually expressions which echo experiences from our childhoods. They are not always easy to recognize because sometimes they hide behind masks of compassion or mock selflessness. They may say, "I'm only telling you this for your own good," or "It's because I love you so much that I'm telling you these things." Keep in mind that most of us have been taught that if a thing can't be quantified scientifically it isn't real, and this certainly throws out the welcome mat for these inner critics.

Inner critics come in as many different versions as there are people. One of the toughest ones is the "perfectionist." Its machinations are particularly insidious. It is the part of us that tries to insist that there is always a "right and proper" way to do things. If you are not doing exactly what this critic believes is "proper," you're in for trouble. You're not walking the line.

This inner critic is tricky for another reason: At its worst it has you looking outside yourself, projecting the judgment and criticisms you are feeling to something or someone in the external world. You decide you don't like the way a certain person is dressed. Or you don't like the way the instructions are laid out on the page. You find a typographical error on the page (god forbid!) Or, if you are in a workshop, you might find yourself correcting the instructor or other participants and feeling quite self-righteous about doing so. If someone calls you on it, you're likely to say that you have a right to your opinions. You are a perfectionist, or you have a highly developed sense of aesthetics, or you simply know more than anyone else in the room. All this might be true but taking that defensive stance keeps you victimized by the perfectionist *virus*.

This kind of critical posturing takes the joy out of life for you and everyone around you. But even more than this, the person with the perfectionist bug always turns upon him- or herself. After all, it is impossible to escape the fact that we ourselves are always, ultimately, the victims of our own worst behavior.

The inner critic that adopts the role of perfectionist is often rewarded in everyday reality because it is usually perceived as a way to "get things done right." While there is an element of truth in this, it is discernment, not perfectionism that allows us to get things done and maintain high standards. In all too many cases the inner critic who harps on perfection turns out to be a crippling influence, preventing the person who is stuck with that bug from accomplishing much of anything–because nothing is ever quite right. In this respect perfectionism is pathological, even when it expresses itself as either a spirit guide or as a critic of the whole notion of spirit guides.

I focus attention on the inner critic who takes the form of a perfectionist because it is a very common syndrome in our society. And it is often the most difficult inner critic to address because it is seen as a virtue, a quality that wins us a sense of authority and control in other peoples' eyes.

Nearly always there is a degree of emotional discomfort or even pain that goes along with the inner critic, whether it takes the form of perfectionist or as the more benign, caring voice that tells you to *be careful*. After all, nobody likes to be criticized or put down, especially not by a person who we may perceive as being bigger, more powerful, or more aggressive than ourselves. And when we feel this discomfort or pain, there's only one thing we want to do–push it away. We want to escape the deprecating eyes of our critic. So what do we usually do? The easiest and most common response is to stop doing the activity that caught the inner critic's attention. When that activity is one that you ordinarily love to do, this reflex robs you of the personal satisfaction you might have otherwise enjoyed.

Reclaiming Your Power

There are many devices described in self-help books for disarming our inner critics. For example, one book advises us to "surround the inner critic with white light." Another says, "send light and love to the inner critic until they stop." Trouble is, the critics don't stop. You may throw a shield of light or love between you and your critic but they are still there. When you least expect it they will slip from behind the shield and make themselves known in some other way.

Just as with real human beings, it is difficult to change the behavior of an inner critic. That doesn't mean that you have to continue to be victimized by them or to hand over your intuitive and creative powers to them. What's the alternative? What do you do when an inner critic keeps popping up in your mind?

First, consider the fact that your main reaction to the discomfort or pain of an attack by an inner critic is fear. And fear is the most primitive emotion in the human experience. When fear is experienced it triggers a specific part of your brain, called the "reptilian," or "old brain." This is the part of our brain that tells us to quickly withdraw when we've put our hand in the fire. And, of course, if we didn't have the services of this part of our brain we would probably never make it through childhood.

In human evolution we have not yet developed the ability to discern the difference between physical pain and emotional pain. We have pretty much the same response to both. We withdraw. But anyone who has been in a loving relationship knows that even those who love us the most do things that cause us pain. If we don't address that pain but letting our loved one know that we've been injured, there is no chance of finding a resolution. Many relationships are destroyed not so much by the original injury as by the inability of the two parties to communicate with each other about it.

What we learn in vital relationships is that wounds fester when not addressed openly and with satisfaction for both parties. That festering deadens the relationship, builds lasting resentment and distrust that is, to say the least, crazy-making. And something very similar to what heals relationships with lovers also can free you of the negative influences of your inner critics.

Embracing What You Fear

The first time I was introduced to this concept was many years ago when I was having trouble with a supervisor in the engineering firm where I was employed. A psychotherapist told me, "If you want to solve this thing you've got to fully embrace the source of your pain."

"Are you crazy? The guy would punch out my lights."

The therapist smiled. "I don't mean literally embrace the person. I mean embrace the fear instead of trying to escape from it. The fear is serving a purpose—or at least your ego thinks it is. You have to discover what that purpose is."

The therapist then had me get in touch with a moment when I was particularly hurt by something my supervisor had said or done. That was easy. Just that morning he had criticized something I'd done in front of the field crew that I supervised, and I'd felt angry and humiliated.

Now I was instructed to close my eyes and focus on exactly what I was feeling. I was not supposed to analyze what was going on or try to change it in any way, shape or form. Just embrace the feelings, be with them. Get to know them.

After a few moments, I was bombarded by imagery from my past. I remembered times in grade school when teachers humiliated me in front of my friends. Admittedly, I was a dreamer and rarely applied myself to my schoolwork, so I am sure my teachers got very impatient with me. But as I relived those experiences I actually felt the weight of my present supervisor's criticism lift from me. Part of what rose up in my consciousness was the realization that as an adult I was not in the same position that I'd been in during my early years. I had a choice about how to respond.

The next day at work I had a meeting with the offending supervisor. I told him that when he "dumped" on me in front of my crew it caused more problems than it solved. I was concerned with getting the job done as quickly and efficiently as possible. So I was asking him to address errors I had made in a less deprecating way. My supervisor's response was curt. "Just do your job right and neither one of us will have a problem."

Now, this wasn't exactly the receptive response I was looking for but I let it go and we both went back to work. In the following days, however, my supervisor had the opportunity to call me on three errors I'd made. In the past, this would have provided him with a lot of ammunition to disgrace me in front of my men. But he didn't do that this time. He pointed out the errors and calmly asked me to fix them. He wasn't all sweetness and light, nor did I require him to be, but the tension soon diminished between us. We never became friends but after this we were at least productive co-workers.

This same process really does work with your inner critic. It works whether the expression of this critic is a vague feeling of self doubt or is as clear as a mental image of the step uncle who was your worst nightmare in your childhood.

If you are feeling doubt or fear, close your eyes, breathe easily and smoothly, and allow yourself to draw closer to that self doubt. Be patient with yourself now because your reflex is to want to pull away, withdrawing from the pain. As we've already said, the chances are that you won't want to get closer. Your reflex will be to escape the source of the pain rather than drawing closer to it or just sitting with it.

What you'll soon discover is that as you let go and allow yourself to be with these feelings you begin to experience increased calm and a sense of being well grounded. If your inner critic is in the form of an image of a person, or perhaps an animal or fantasy figure, you can even start to have a little fun with it. Here I recall a story told by a woman in one of our workshops. Her worst and most powerful inner critic, her mother, who showed up in her dreams as a roaring lion.

As this woman sat with her pain, remembering how her mother had criticized her for nearly everything, she asked this fearsome inner critic, "Why are you in my life? What are you trying to teach me?" As soon as she asked this question, the lion literally laid down at her feet, and in an instant was transformed into a timid rabbit. A rabbit! All these years, the woman realized, her mother's fears had driven her actions toward her daughter. This realization was greatly liberating. Thereafter, whenever that inner critic roared like a lion, the woman could see the timid rabbit behind the roar. At times she even had imaginary conversations with the rabbit, thus learning more about her inner critic and how to handle it.

In creativity seminars that we teach, we often have

people write a story that satirizes their inner critics. The same trick might work for you here. The goal is to keep the critic in character but put them in positions where they look ridiculous and where the character defects that make them so mean are revealed for all to see.

Some of these stories have been raucously funny, some quite sad. The end result, though, is that by writing or even thinking about these little scenarios, our inner critics are no longer quite the threats they once were. It's a little like facing your own demons. Not until you've truly faced and acknowledged them will you ever be able to come to terms with them. Once acknowledged we find ways to liberate ourselves from the destructive hold they have on us. The path to that new freedom might be unveiled by the processes described in this book, by attending a workshop that addresses the issue you're facing, or by working with a counselor.

When we at last face our inner critics we stand a chance of discovering why we fear them. As often as not we discover that behind the lion's roar is the timid whimper of a rabbit. ~

Journeying for Spirit Guides

*The more knowledge we acquire
the more mystery we find...
~Albert Einstein*

In the past few years, there has been increasing interest in Earth-centered spiritual practices, be it Native American, Celtic, African, Siberian or Aboriginal. Part of the reason for this is that these early traditions were based on deeply personal and intimate connections with the natural world and many of us today long for that kind of relationship in light of today's busy, fast-paced life styles. The ancient peoples made sense of their lives not so much through analytical methods, as we do today, as through their intuitive abilities and their direct experiences with the spirit world. Their intuitive capacities allowed them to appreciate the spiritual essence not only of each other but of the plants they ate, the animals they hunted, and the influences beyond the physical realm, such as the stars, the moon, and the weather. They lived according to the rhythms of nature and watched all the beings around them for lessons in living.

To get a taste of the kind of world they lived in, imagine what it was like 10,000 or more years ago. With no electrical lights their night world was illuminated only by the stars, the moon, and perhaps an occasional campfire or makeshift lantern. Whatever stores of food they might have had were meager, at best. Most of their food was freshly picked or freshly killed, requiring that they hunt, fish, or gather their foods as they required and as their immediate environment provided. And while they might have rustic structures or caves to shelter them from storms, they mostly had to adjust their activities to the seasons, which they observed carefully.

The artifacts and other anthropological records left behind by ancient peoples reveal that they experienced themselves as inseparable from nature and spirit, that is, as a contiguous part of it. All that surrounded them was of one Source, and even the empty spaces between were perceived as part of that creation within which they took part. Imagine the planet without even the most rudimentary man-made technologies and you might be able to get a sense of how it was possible to feel so interconnected with all and everything. Imagine sitting under the stars at night, thousands of years before the internal combustion engine--no airplanes flying overhead, no refrigerator motors humming away in the kitchen, no radios blaring or TV sets flashing the latest news. The silence itself was profound, interrupted only by the calls of animals or the occasional murmur of the human voice. Indeed, one wonders if it would have been possible, even a few hundred years ago, to literally hear the music of the spheres and find our bodies instinctively responding to its rhythms as we went about our lives. This was a world where the inner messages of intuition had little or no competition.

Certainly in this early world, it would have been much easier than it is today to directly experience the subtle spiritual influences all around us. Truly, it would have been abundantly evident that we were the children of Mother Earth and Father Sky. She provided the womb, the soil for the seeds that would grow and nurture us, and nurture the animals that in turn provided us with food, and with fur to protect us when the weather turned cold. He, Father Sky, provided the rain and the sunshine that allowed the seeds to grow.

If the traditional stories, songs and rituals, many of them still in existence today, are any indication, spirit guides, in a variety of forms, were as much a part of early people's lives as were the fully incarnate members of their own families and their fellow villagers. There were spirit guides to counsel when to plant corn, when and where to hunt, where and when to move on to other areas, and what kind of "medicine" would be required to find solution to problems of daily living.

Rituals and dances provided the earliest peoples with ways of both expressing and experiencing their spirituality. In dances they might move with the tranquil rhythms of a quiet meadow or with the roaring violence of a great electrical storm. They might move like the hunter stalking his prey, or like the lion standing his ground against the hunters with their spears and menacing feints. They might enter a space of deep contemplation, and from this space get in touch with the memories of ancestors hundreds of years in the past. Or their dances might imitate the movements of giving birth, helping to induce an expectant mother or educate young women.

Anthropologists called these early rituals "trance-dances," since as an outside observer from the modern world such rituals might appear to be some sort of madness, where the mind appears to have taken leave. What we now know, however, from having done our homework, witnessed these ancient rituals and even entered into them with open hearts, is that they represent profound ways of learning about ourselves, our inner life, and our relationships to the cosmos. Copying the movements of an animal in flight, for instance, or copying the movements of a mountain lion as it hunted its prey, taught the shaman the meaning of awe or the hunter the skills of his vocation. Humans learned their lessons of the Earth at a cellular level, offering a powerful spiritual connection that taught respect for all of Creation.

Whether the spiritual entity was an animal form, a human form, a plant form, or even the form of a more tenuous form such as the force of the wind, the force of lightning, or the force that caused the corn to grow, each had its individual lessons. Sometimes the early peoples made small hand held objects that, precursors of the icons of later religions, to honor their spirit helpers. Sometimes called "fetishes," after the European word "fete," that is, *celebration*, these objects literally did that–consecrating these entities.

The objects themselves were sometimes held or used as personal adornments, constant reminders of the important spiritual roles played by these etheric beings.

One of the most powerful spiritual techniques that we've adopted from our ancient ancestors is what has come to be called "journeying." Even today, journeying is practiced as a way to make contact with spirit helpers. The process is actually quite simple. The journeyer usually works with an assistant who holds a steady beat with a small hand drum or rattle. The beat of the drum or rattle induces a somewhat altered state of consciousness, while keeping the journeyer aware of everyday consciousness. In this slightly altered consciousness state, the person easily travels into dream space, where she meets her spirit guide.

Prior to this ritual, the shaman or other teacher has given the journeyer instructions. Usually this involved suggestions to imagine being in the forest, or perhaps in the mountains, or at the seashore, where the journeyer might encounter some signal that they were at the beginning of a secret path. They would then take this path, following it along and noting the terrain as they went. At some point, sometimes after encountering and overcoming certain hazards, one would come to a clearing in the forest, a natural formation such as a rock, a cave, or a hollowed out tree, or perhaps even a man-made structure, where he would stop. This would be the place where one would meet their spirit guide.

After greetings and an exchange of introductions, the journeyer might tell the guide why she had taken this journey and how she wished the spirit guide might aid her. The guide might then take the journeyer further along their path, deeper into the mountain environment, woods or whatever other place they were in. And along the way, the guide might decide to point out certain things to the journeyer, or even counsel them in some way.

All during the journey, the drummer, who might at this point seem to the journeyer to be miles away, would maintain the steady, monotonous beat of the drum or rattle. This helps the person concentrate on her journey and helps to mark the entry point of the journey. As one person commented, "It's like the drummer is sitting at the trail head, sending me a signal so that I can find my way back."

As the journey begins, I try to hold a rhythm somewhere between 150 and 200 beats per minute. This may vary, depending on the environment and the participants. For example, if there is background noise such as traffic, or even distant voices, I find it is helpful to maintain the faster rhythm, say 200 beats per minute or slightly more. Slower rhythms tend to induce a more tranquil state of mind, one where even subtle, external distractions can be disconcerting and pull the person out of this special meditative frame of mind. Contrariwise, if the environment is extremely quiet, such as you might find in more remote wilderness areas, and the person or persons participating are rested and alert, the slower rhythms are often better to work with.

People often ask, can they journey alone? The

answer is yes, though you will need to have a recording of appropriate drumming to play in the background, or a metronome set at 200 up to 250 beats per minute. With practice, you may also find that you can drum or rattle, and journey at the same time, though this is a bit of a challenge at first.

The best drum recordings I've found are those sold by Michael Harner specifically for the journeying process. Check out his website, listed at the end of this chapter, or order by mail. If you have a drum or rattle, and a recorder, you can, of course, record yourself and play it back for your own journey.

The drumming tape should hold the rhythm for about 10 to 15 minutes, after which it pauses, followed by fast drumming for about 3 minutes, calling you back to everyday reality.

Preparations: Make arrangements with a friend who can drum or rattle, or set yourself up with a metronome or drum recording to hold the rhythm for you, as we've just discussed. Use the following narration to put together a mental visualization that you will follow once you get started. Do not depend on the drummer to read this narrative for you since you will want to allow your imagination to carry you freely into dream-space. You do not need to memorize it. Just recall whatever you can. Your memories of the narration will carry you into a scenario that may be quite different from the following. Trust what your mind brings to you:

As the drumming begins, imagine yourself at the head of a trail. You may be able to see only 30 or 40 feet of the trail ahead. As you start out on this journey, more and more details come to your attention–for example, waves, birds and driftwood if you are at the seashore, flora if you are in a forest, cliffs in the mountains, or any other scenery appropriate to your imagined environment. Take time to do this, for the more detailed your physical surroundings, the more real your journey will become.

Now imagine yourself finding and following a trail. Note details such as the elevation of the trail, what it looks like at the right or left of the path, whether or not the trail is clear, worn, or rather faintly marked. Notice the sky overhead, any natural sounds, the temperature of the air, your own feelings.

After some hiking, you will come to a place of rest where you will meet your spirit guide. This might be a clearing in the forest, a ledge outside a cave, a resting place in the desert, perhaps a log at a special place on the beach. Make yourself comfortable in this place.

As you wait, you may hear someone approaching. You may wish to stand and greet them as they arrive. You exchange greetings and introductions. Then you tell this guide why you have come on this journey and what you wish from them. They may answer either in words (usually it will just seem like thoughts coming into your mind) or by some gesture which will have meaning for you.

The guide may now take you further on your journey, where he or she broadens your awareness either by showing you something, putting you into a particular situation, or literally by talking with you or offering you intuitive insights (which come automatically and wordlessly.)

At some point you become aware that you have gotten everything you have come for, at least at this point. It is time to return to your everyday existence. This is marked by the drumming becoming rapid, as if calling you back.

Slowly open your eyes, look around, ground yourself by checking out at least three physical objects in the room where you are.

You may now want to record your experiences in your journal.

Map of The Journey

1. Choose a time of day and a place where you will not be disturbed for at least 30 minutes.

2. Have a helper who can drum, a metronome, or your own prepared recording of a drum.

3. Lie down on the floor, perhaps with a pillow under your head. Do not get so comfortable that you will fall asleep.

4. When you are ready, start the drumming and let yourself remember the preliminary narrative of the journey. Let your mind carry you on the journey, but do not worry about following the above narrative to the letter. That narrative is only a statement of general intent. It is important to allow your mind to drift, carrying you along on perhaps a very different journey than you anticipated. This is the true value of the

journey, to carry you to places in your inner world that you may or may not realize are there.

5. As the drumming turns to the faster pace that calls you back, say goodbye to your guide, thank him or her for her help and concern, then turn away and come back down the path to your starting point. (*Note: if you are using a metronome, you will need a timer to tell you when your time is up.*)

6. Slowly open your eyes. Check out the room, then record your journey in a journal or notebook.

After the Journey

About half the people doing this journey get animals as teachers and guides. But spirit guides, as you already know, can take many different forms–from human beings to beams of light, or simply subtle inner voices.

Understand that the guides you get while journeying can be employed in whatever way you wish. You need not go through the journeying process to contact them. From time to time, however, a journeying session can be tremendously revealing, opening up new areas of your consciousness and awakening the deepest powers of your intuition. ~

---

* *Michael Harner offers several journeying CDs. I recommend "Shamanic Journey Double Drumming." Check the internet for his current contact information.*

Choices on the Spiritual Path

One then wonders whether his spirits are merely pieces of the unconscious or is the unconscious simply a reflection of this interaction with spirits? That is, which is the more substantive reality—the unconscious or the world of spirits? ...I think these two are the same.
~ Wilson Van Dusen, *"A Confirmation of Swedenborg in Recent Empirical Findings"*

As I was putting together this, the newest edition of *Spirit Guides,* I found myself reviewing quotes from other books and writings that I'd collected over the years. I also found notes from readers, some with questions, others with comments that I had always meant to incorporate into a book. While reviewing these I felt compelled to add one more chapter to this book.

Some of the more common questions arising were: How do we determine the value or credibility of something my spirit guides tell me? How do we gauge the intent of a particular spirit guide, and why have the particular guides that communicate with us become a part of our lives? Have we attracted them through our own actions or inner processes, or have we been drawn into their realm? Is the guidance they are giving us of a higher order—or possibly a lower one? And then there is the ongoing debate about whether our guides are products of our unconscious minds or if they are separate from us, beings with their own individual identities.

On the last question, you might recall our previous discussion of Carl Jung and his conviction that the spirit guides "have their own life" and "represented a force which was not myself." Similarly, writers like Helen Schucman of *A Course in Miracles* fame, and Jane Roberts of the *Seth Speaks* series of books, presented convincing evidence that Jung's observation was right, that the spirit beings with whom they communicated had their own lives and represented a force beyond the writer's singular life.

In the epigram at the start of this chapter, this issue is addressed in a slightly different way. I quote Wilson Van Dusen, a highly respected contemporary psychologist and researcher, who speaks of his interest in the work of Emanuel Swedenborg, the 18th century Swedish philosopher, theologian, metaphysician, spiritualist and scientist. Van Dusen rhetorically asks if the spirits that influence our lives are "pieces of the unconscious or is the unconscious simply a reflection of this interaction with spirits?" His conclusion: "I think these two are the same." If we subscribe to the belief that *all is One*, or that *All and Everything is of a unified whole*, how could we see it any other way: within this larger perception of Creation there is no separation between spirit and human consciousness.

Van Dusen's statement appears, at first glance, to contradict what Jung said about his spirit guide Philemon, that his spirit guide *represented a force separate from him*. This is one of the great paradoxes of spiritual understanding. But it need not be a source of conflict in our minds if we recognize that the unified whole we call Creation contains within it infinite diversity and individuation.

One of Swedenborg's great contributions was his perception that each of our lives depends on our relationships with a hierarchy of spirits; throughout our lives, and whether we are aware of it or not, these spiritual forces flow into our feelings and into the matrix of our thoughts and actions. Much of the time, we see no boundaries between ourselves and these spirits; they appear to merge with us. Until we develop an awareness of these spiritual forces as having their own existence independent of us, and develop skills for handling our relationships with them, they may quite freely live out their beings through us. It is very easy to go through our lives believing that all of what we think and feel, all of our feelings, thoughts and actions, are simply our own; it takes a special awareness of the kind Swedenborg describes to see that our relations to the world of spirits is not unlike our everyday relations with the people around us.

Through Swedenborg's lens of perception we see all of life as a hicrarchy of different orders of spirits, from the lowest to the highest, interacting with one another. He describes humanity as the free space or meeting ground of all these hierarchies. Essentially, good forces and their opposite rule through this hierarchy down to us humans, who stand in the free space. And then it is out of our choices and experiences that we identify with the spiritual forces from everywhere within that hierarchy. Our very lives are thus the result of these choices and their influences on us. In *The Importance of Individuals*, William James says, "Tell him to live by yes and no—yes to everything good, no to everything bad." Those who acknowledge themselves as receptacles of all that is good, including the power to think and to feel, tends toward the good side; at the opposite pole, those who acknowledge themselves as receptacles of the evil tend to live accordingly.

Because of the profound importance of our choices, our individuation, that is, our ability to experience our separate identities, is at least as important in our spiritual relations as it is with our human ones. We know how the lack of individuation works in our everyday human interactions: If we merge emotionally with another person, our spouse or other loved one, for example, we may begin to feel lost, without a clear identity of our own. We may find ourselves unable to say or know how we feel or what we think or what we want; our own life experience is so enmeshed with the other person's that we do not recognize where one stops and the other begins. This is one of the great puzzles of loving and caring for others. How do we love and care for others, establishing true intimacy, and still maintain a clear sense of ourselves? So many of life's conflicts, and even tragedies, arise from this apparently uniquely human puzzle. We see it in our conflicts and disappointments involving ourselves and our life partners, with our children, with our friends, with our communities, and certainly with our countries, when the other's actions or viewpoints suddenly reveal that we do not share the same feelings, thoughts, beliefs or loyalties that we'd become so dependent upon.

Merging with others is part of the human experience and an essential part of our social evolution. It becomes problematic only when we are unable to experience our individual lives, when we blindly adopt the thoughts and feelings of the other person and mistake them as our own. Because spiritual forces don't manifest in physical form we often accept them as simply extensions of ourselves, perhaps even perceive them as our own expressions, knowledge or insights. Van Dusen states: "In modern terms one would say spirits are in the unconscious and there live out their desires in what is to man the origin of his thought and feeling." During a workshop on spirit guides that I was teaching some years ago, we had been discussing the subtleties of the merging process when an older man said, "This tells me that who we consort with in the spiritual realm is at least as important as who we consort with in our everyday lives." And, of course, this is true, an awareness that Swedenborg would be sure to support.

While we may well possess free will, if we're to have full and satisfying lives we need to take responsibility for our own feelings, beliefs and actions. We need to individuate, to learn the boundaries between ourselves and others, to experience and respect our separateness, even as we recognize our participation in the greater Oneness. This is a common understanding in both psychology and spiritual development. But we can have a complete picture of what this means only by looking carefully at our relation to the hierarchy of spirits that has conditioned us. To simplify, consider a person who associates primarily with lower spirits, ones that are constantly berating others, ones who have no respect for others' lives, either on the spiritual or the everyday human level. Generally such people and spirits assert themselves largely through fear and willful domination for the purpose of bending others to their wishes. They call for us to conform to their beliefs or to a preconceived structure they are advocating, rather than calling for and welcoming our participation. Correspondingly, the person who associates with the lower forces in this way will reflect those same attitudes in his thoughts, feelings and actions toward himself. He'll most likely be self-centered, self-critical (though this is often hidden in arrogance), controlling, negative, manipulative and willful, nearly always focused on what's wrong with the world. Viewed from a more compassionate perspective, such a person suffers from an unremitting sense of aloneness and alienation, inadequacy (often masked in greed, envy and jealousy), feeling himself to be a potential victim of other people's will or external circumstances (thus his desperate need for control).

It is easy to be drawn to spirits of a lower order. They may get our attention by berating us, by pointing out our shortcomings or failings, or the shortcomings and failings of others, usually in the name of improving ourselves. They may obsessively point to the horrors of life on our planet—to war, murder and mayhem as irrefutable proof of the wrong thinking of others or even as evidence of how evil some person, regime, group, way of thinking, or humanity itself is. Carried to extremes, we see this mechanism exploited by despots like Adolph Hitler. They find power by seeking scapegoats to blame for the "disorder" of the world, then rally support for destroying those "evil forces," promising that when their task is completed order will be restored and all will live in harmony. Nearly always, campaigns such as this are expressed in terms of fighting for the common good and to make the world a better place. Are there ever truly righteous causes, ideals or compassionate or higher causes we should champion? Certainly there are but as Mohandas Gandhi famously pointed out, "pursuit of truth did not permit violence being inflicted on one's opponent...nonviolence and truth are inseparable."

The spirits that espouse the lower forces are as difficult to ignore as a car wreck. That which shocks our senses and arouses the most primitive reactions of our brains has a powerful attraction. It is from this that journalists have coined the phrase, "If it bleeds, it leads!"

However hypnotic the lower forces might seem to be, the bottom line is that we always have a choice about consorting with them. A spirit guide, for example, might keep after us day after day, urging us to turn on the news or a site on the internet that hammers us with how bad things are, immersing us in stories of the latest crooked politician or human catastrophe. This is literally entertaining and being entertained by the lower forces. It is not that we must deny that such evils exist, or that we inure ourselves to compassion for human suffering, or that we should not keep up with current events, but we do need to recognize our own relation to the lower forces that may have come to be so dominate in our lives.

Swedenborg's teachings suggest that just as we experience ourselves as being independent of the spirits, the spirits experience themselves as independent from us. Or, as Van Dusen says, "Each, man or spirit, is given to feel he is free and (that he) rules." This is important to recognize since it is only through recognizing our separateness, and our unique boundaries, that we can experience relationship and respect for the other's individual identity, be it a spiritual source or human. Merged, relationship dissolves. The philosopher Martin Buber, in his book *I and Thou*, points out that only through our recognition of the other as having an existence independent of ours can there be a dialog between us. Only then can we make choices that say, this is how I feel, this is what I think, this is how I experience the world, and I respect that you are different. Only through this recognition of the I and the Thou can we love, make choices, develop compassion, work out ways of communicating more constructively, or learn ways to defend and fight should that become necessary. And again, paradoxically, it is only through our full recognition of our unique separateness that we can experience that common ground where we are one.

The order of the spiritual hierarchy that Swedenborg speaks of ranges from the lower to the higher, each of which can be recognized by the behavior and the obvious intent behind the spirits' words and deeds. Dr. Van Dusen describes the lower order as "irreligious or anti-religious," often interfering with the person's spiritual or religious practices by mocking them or acting contemptuously toward that person for taking such beliefs and practices seriously. We might also experience this lower order of spirit as our own self-doubts or even self-derision.

It should be noted that we might or might not experience this force as a voice or being separate from us. As often as not it shows up as feeling depressed or bad about ourselves, as a focus on our own perceived failures, as a lack of faith, or even something as seemingly external as our profound dismay with the hostile or "dysfunctional" world we live in. Frequently, we are able to point to a "cause," or cite spiritual or physically *objective evidence* for feeling or believing as we do. Just as we need to pay attention to the objective reality of gravity while we live in this fragile human form, so we need to pay attention to the objective reality that there may be others in the world who do not always have our best interests at heart.

Swedenborg tells us that all that we experience can be thought of as spiritual, that *"the spiritual world cannot be separated from the natural, nor the natural world from the spiritual."*

Paraphrasing Swedenborg, Van Dusen says, "Good spirits or angels dwell in the most interior aspects of man's mind—in his loves, affections...they think more abstractly. One of their thoughts would cover thousands of a natural man's thoughts. The soul, spirit or interior man are the same thing."

One of the ways we have of identifying higher forces or spirits is that the higher forces are usually quiet beings, far quieter than the typically verbose and occasionally manic and assertive lower spirits. The higher spirits are generally associated with patience, serenity, and respect. A friend once described the character of her spirit guide as "a woman of few words but smooth, flowing and lovingly imperturbable power." Higher spirits are associated with a way of being that is inclusive, oceanic, reciprocally loving and caring, compassionate, and empathetic, remembering always to extend this same caring to themselves. They radiate well being and connectedness with a higher order that's infinite, ineffable...beyond the reach of words. We perhaps most commonly think of higher forces being angels, who come to assist a person during a crisis or a near disaster.

Swedenborg suggests that we can recognize the higher spirits by their respect for all of life, for their recognition of limitless diversity and *differentness*, for their apparent acceptance of chaos and disorder, and a recognition that even the violent and grievous forces are enveloped by a larger and greater order that is beyond our comprehension. Gandhi spoke of the *love force* or *soul force*. Again, Van Dusen says, "They reside in the interior mind which does not think in words but universals which comprise many particulars... Many of the higher order are purely visual and use no words at all." When we are in touch with the higher order of spirits we tend to be more focused on the inner world, with little or no attachment to material ideas or things. We have little or no interest in memories, pleasant ones or not such pleasant ones, as we are in what Eckhart Tolle has called the Now, or on universal wisdom (that which applies to all equally).

A favorite writer of mine, Abraham Maslow, helps to shed light on how it might feel to encounter the higher forces when he speaks of "those all-too-few moments of self-affirmation which we call *peak experiences.*"

By learning to recognize the characteristics of the higher and lower spirits, we can stop at any moment in our lives and ask ourselves what we are experiencing. What counsel or spiritual influence captured our attention? It does not matter that we feel the force coming from outside us, or as the result of our own best reasoning or objective observations. They are still manifestations of spiritual forces no matter how they may be manifest, for as Wilson Van Deusen points out, "pieces of the unconscious and the world of spirits are the same."

How we experience our lives is determined largely by our relationships to these spiritual forces and the choices we make around them. In Dr. Van Dusen's words, "one would say spirits are in the unconscious and there live out their desires in what is to man the origin of his thoughts and feelings. In the normal situation man is not aware of their action, taking it to be his own thought and feeling." Our lives are thus determined by the relations we choose with these spiritual forces—higher or lower.

In Robert A. Johnson's *Inner Work: Using Dreams & Active Imagination for Personal Growth*, he speaks of make-believe journeys we can take through active imagination, during which we may encounter spiritual forces. He says, "If you find yourself meeting an inner guide and being led off on a mythical adventure, it will help if you understand that this is a legitimate and excellent way to live out parts of yourself that can't be lived fully in your immediate, daily, physical life."

One of the more interesting authors in my small library of channeled books is a writer by the name of Andrew Ramer. In his book *Revelations for a New Millennium: Saintly and Celestial Prophecies of Joy and Renewal*, he says, "Today not everyone hears voices, not everyone is open to the inflow of cosmic consciousness. But in the future, all of us will be open in this way, all of us will be prophets and sibyls... Then we will not need anyone else to tell us how to live our lives, any more than we will need anyone else to tell us how to fix our stove. For all of us will be living in balance, harmony, and connection."

Whether we perceive ourselves as receiving counsel or guidance from an entity or spirit guide that is clearly not ourselves, be it human or spiritual, or we are focusing on following our own inner counsel, the question to ask ourselves is always the same: From where on the spiritual hierarchy from lower to higher do these thoughts, feelings and intentions come? And what, within that hierarchy of forces, will our words or deeds contribute to what we presume to be the evolving consciousness of our planet? ~

Bibliography

Angel Answers, and *Revelations for a New Millennium,* by Andrew Ramer, Harper Collins

The Father Reaches of Human Nature, by A.H. Maslow

The Holotropic Mind: The Three Levels of Consciousness and How They Shape Our Lives, by Stanislav Grof, M.D. with Hal Zina Bennett, Harper Collins

The Importance of Individuals, by William James

Intuition Magic: Understanding Your Psychic Nature, by Linda Keen

The Last Ghost Dance: A Guide for Earth Mages, by Brooke Medicine Eagle

The Magical Approach: Seth Speaks About the Art of Creative Living, by Jane Roberts

Memories, Dreams, Reflections, by C.G. Jung, Vintage Books

The Presence of Other Worlds, by Wilson Van Dusen

The Way of the Shaman, by Michael Harner

About the Authors

Hal Zina Bennett is the author of more than 35 successful fiction and non-fiction books. He is a student of shamanism and metaphysics. He is available for lectures and seminars. His email address is: Halbooks@HalZinaBennett.com. Website address: www.HalzinaBennett.Com

Susan J Sparrow is the co-author of *Spirit Guides* and *Follow Your Bliss*. She is a teacher, reading specialist, gardener, knitter and book publishing consultant. Her email address is: Write@Pacific.Net

—062010ED4PRINT6

Made in the USA
San Bernardino, CA
15 August 2016